MONEY, SEX & POWER

Also by the same author:

CELEBRATION OF DISCIPLINE
STUDY GUIDE FOR CELEBRATION OF DISCIPLINE
FREEDOM OF SIMPLICITY
STUDY GUIDE TO MONEY, SEX & POWER

MONEY, SEX & POWER

The challenge of the Disciplined Life

Richard J. Foster

HODDER & STOUGHTON
LONDON SYDNEY AUCKLAND TORONTO

In memory of David M. Leach

faithful minister of Christ and

dear friend to our family

Unless otherwise indicated, all scriptual quotations are from the
Revised Standard Version of the bible.

British Library Cataloguing in Publication Data

Foster, Richard J.
   Money, sex and power: the challenge of the disciplined life.
   1. Christian Life
   I. Title
   248.4   BV4501.2

ISBN 0 340 41393 X

Designed by Don Hatch

CONTENTS

ACKNOWLEDGMENTS

The sacrifice my family has endured to see this book to completion is considerable. My heartfelt thanks to Carolynn, my wife, who bore the burden with me and gave me many insightful suggestions that have made the book far better than it would have been otherwise. Joel and Nathan, our children, were exceedingly understanding through the obsessive months of writing. Nathan, especially, sacrificed our reading time together at night—happily, I can now return to this as well as many other family joys.

Lynda Graybeal, my associate, has done far more than enter, print out, and proofread the manuscript. She has been an invaluable source of wisdom. Many of her comments opened up whole new creative directions for the book.

Some years back I spoke at a retreat outside of Washington, D.C., sponsored by The Ministry of Money, and it was there that I met the director, Don McClanan. It was through Don that I first saw the connection between the money-sex-power issue and the monastic vows; I am indebted to him.

Kathy Gaynor, reference librarian at Friends University, was especially helpful in my research. She found "unfindable" books with amazing speed, at times scouring the countryside for an obscure reference. My thanks to her.

Over the months, I read the entire manuscript to a literary group here at Friends University of which I am a member. They made many useful suggestions. Several others read all or part of the manuscript, and their comments helped me a great deal. They include Vivian Felix, George Fooshee, David Holley, and Richard Sosnowski. Roy M. Carlisle, my editor at Harper & Row, San Francisco, has been deeply involved in the development of this book from the first day I mentioned it to him as an embryonic idea several years ago. I have appreciated his patience and encouragement.

This is my known list of indebtedness. There are many others who have helped me write this book who will forever remain unknown. A phrase here or an experience there has sharpened my thinking and created a new idea. I could never trace these ideas to their sources, for they have merged with the flow of ideas from a thousand others. But even if I cannot thank everyone individually, I can express indebtedness—and I do.

PREFACE

A special concern has surrounded the writing of this book. To the popular mind, topics like prayer and worship carry an aura of spirituality, whereas the themes of money, sex, and power sound terribly "secular" at best. My longing throughout the writing has been to help people sense that as we come to these "secular" issues we are treading on holy ground. To live rightly with reference to money and sex and power is to live sacramentally. To misuse and abuse these is to desecrate the holy things of God.

I have sought to write in a spirit of reverence and worship, knowing that I was handling sacred themes. Each day of the writing I began with a time of meditation upon one of the psalms, and in this way I read through the entire psalter. My desire was to be baptized into the hopes and aspirations of the psalm writers, for the psalter is the prayer book of the Church. With the cadence of joy and beauty, worship and adoration that comes from the psalms I was able to look with new eyes at the issues of money, sex, and power. Then, and only then, was I prepared to write on these themes that are so close to the heart of God. My hope and prayer is that reading these words will help you as the writing of them has helped me.

I should, at the outset, note the special problem of the personal pronoun when referring to God. I think it is obvious to all that God is not a male deity as opposed to a female deity. God is beyond and includes our distinctions of sexuality. As long ago as the 14th-century, Juliana

Juliana of Norwich declared, "As truly as God is our Father, so truly is God our Mother." The Bible is full of both feminine and masculine imagery for God. However, when we come to the personal pronoun for God, it is difficult to express God's greatness in this regard. The problem is not with God, but with us. Our language is simply too limited. The attempt to solve this problem with dashes and slashes is semantically awkward and aesthetically abhorrent. I have, therefore, chosen to follow the standard usage of the masculine pronoun "he" and "him", although I am keenly aware of the inadequacies of this approach.

Richard J. Foster
February 1985
Friends University

1. Money, Sex and Power in Christian Perspective

> It is vanity to seek riches that shall perish and to put one's hope in them. It is vanity also to aspire to honours and to climb to high degree. It is vanity to follow the lust of the flesh.
>
> —THOMAS à KEMPIS

The crying need today is for people of faith to live faithfully. This is true in all spheres of human existence, but is particularly true with reference to money, sex, and power. No issues touch us more profoundly or more universally. No themes are more inseparably intertwined. No topics cause more controversy. No human realities have greater power to bless or to curse. No three things have been more sought after or are more in need of a Christian response.

The issues of money, sex, and power catapult us into the arena of moral choice. In this book I am seeking to describe how we are to live ethically, but I am not attempting to cover the waterfront of ethical inquiry, as one might do in a textbook on ethics. Instead, by dealing with three issues of such importance in modern society I hope to give clues for how we, as followers of Christ, are to handle the many ethical choices we must face daily.

In doing this I believe I am following the pattern of Christ himself. Jesus did not give detailed instruction on how we are to live in every corner of life. Instead he took the crucial issues of his day and showed how the gospel message bears upon them. And in this way he gave us paradigms for conjugating the many other verbs of ethical choice.

Jesus gave considerable attention to the themes of money, sex, and power. Of the three, he spoke more about money and power than he did about sex, for the simple reason that sex was not the burning issue then that it has become in our day. Today, however, we must deal vigorously with the sex issue for there is obvious misery in modern society from a lack of subordination of eros to agape.

WHY MONEY, SEX AND POWER?

You may well wonder why I would choose to write a book on the specific topics of money, sex, and power. The answer is simple. Throughout history, and in our own experience, these issues seem inseparably intertwined. Money manifests itself as power. Sex is used to acquire both money and power. And power is often called "the best aphrodisiac." We could discuss at length the interlacing connections. There is, for example, an important relationship between sex and poverty: sex is the poor man's holiday and the poor woman's disaster. Note also the connection between power and wealth: power is frequently used to manipulate wealth, and wealth is used just as frequently to buy power. And on it goes. The truth is that it is not really possible (or even desirable) to unravel all the intricate ways money, sex, and power intertwine.

Another reason for writing on these themes is that the need is great today. We have gone through upheavals in our culture with regard to each of these issues. The time is right for an attempt to respond to the money—sex—power question. Christians need a fresh articulation of what it means to live faithfully in these areas, and those who are considering the Christian faith deserve some indication of what they might expect if they become followers of Christ.

I have a third reason for writing about these themes. Historically it seems spiritual revivals have been accompanied by a clear, bold response to the issues of money, sex, and power. This is true whether we think of the Benedictine movement, the Franciscan movement, the Cistercian movement, the Reformation movement, the Methodist movement, the modern missionary movement, or any number of other groups. When these revivals occur in a culture, there is a renewal of both devotional experience and ethical life. We need a modern-day renewal of spiritual experience that is ethically potent.

SOCIAL IMPLICATIONS

It is important right at the outset that we see the far-reaching social implications of the issues with which we are dealing. These are matters that profoundly affect corporate and institutional, as well as private, life. The social dimension to money is "business"; for sex it is "marriage"; for power it is "government."[1]*

I am using the terms *business, marriage,* and *government* in their broadest sense. Business refers to the task of bringing forth the goods and services of the earth either to bless or oppress humankind. Marriage refers to the human relationship par excellence that creates the context for either the deepest possible intimacy or the greatest possible alienation. Government refers to the enterprise of human organization that can lead toward either liberty or tyranny. Instantly you can sense that money, sex, and power are vital issues, not only to each of us as individuals, but to all human society.

Business, marriage, and government can be either a supreme benefit or a plague of monstrous proportions.

---

* All strictly bibliographical information is placed in the Notes at the back of the book. Other commentary notes are placed at the bottom of the individual pages.

And the variables that tip the scale one way or the other are more numerous and more complex than merely the character of the individuals involved. Our problems will not be solved simply by getting the "right" kind of people in business or government. That is certainly a good thing, but it does not guarantee that these institutions will serve humankind. Inherent within the institutional structures themselves are destructive forces that need to be transformed by the power of God if they are to benefit human society.

THEMES OF THE CENTURIES

Money, sex, and power are three of the great ethical themes that have concerned human beings throughout the centuries. It was these three things that Dostoevsky dealt with so sensitively in his masterpiece *The Idiot*.[2] In this novel the Christ-figure, Prince Myshkin, is thrust into a culture obsessed with wealth, power, and sexual conquest. But the prince himself has no pride, no greed, no malice, no envy, no vanity, and no fear. His behavior is so abnormal that people do not know what to think of him. They trust him because of his innocence and simplicity, yet his lack of ulterior motives causes them to conclude that he is an idiot.

Skillfully Dostoevsky weaves the themes of money, sex, and power through the story, contrasting the spirit of the prince with all those around him. Of him, the narrator notes, "He did not care for pomp or wealth, nor even for public esteem, but cared only for the truth!"[3] In a letter, Dostoevsky himself said of the prince, "My intention is to portray a truly beautiful soul."[4]

The aristocratic society of Dostoevsky's time could not comprehend an individual like Prince Myshkin, but then neither can modern society. Imagine Myshkin making a guest appearance in a television soap opera. The script writers simply would not know what to do with a person who had no desire for possessions, no craving for sexual conquest, no need for domination.

Of course, the real question throughout the novel is, Who really is the idiot? Perhaps the true fool is the person whose life is dominated by greed and power and sexual conquest.

Of course, Dostoevsky is only representative of a long line of individuals and groups who have given serious and sustained attention to the themes of money, sex, and power. Virtually every major thinker and every great movement have wrestled with these issues. The ancient monastic vows of poverty, chastity, and obedience were a direct response to the issues of money, sex, and power. Or think of the Puritans, who answered the question with their emphasis upon industry, faithfulness, and order. We can learn much by giving attention to their efforts.

THE HISTORIC VOWS: MONEY

Compulsive extravagance is a modern mania. The contemporary lust for "more, more, more" is clearly psychotic; it has completely lost touch with reality. The chasm between Third World poverty and First World affluence is accelerating at an alarming rate. And many earnest believers are at a loss to know what to do in the midst of these perplexing realities.

The monastic response to money is seen in the ancient vow of *poverty*. Intense renunciation was their way of shouting no to the prevailing values of their society. They were, however, giving far more than a negative word. They were saying no in order to say yes. They renounced possessions in order to learn detachment.

The lovable (and sometimes frustrating) Franciscan Brother Juniper had so learned the meaning of detachment that many thought he was a fool. On one occasion he came across an elaborate altar that had silver ringlets hanging from the frontal. He took one look at them and announced, "These ringlets are superfluous," and proceeded to cut them off and give them to the poor. The village priest, of course, was outraged. Poor Juniper simply could not understand the priest's anger, for he assumed he had done him a great service by freeing him from this "display of worldly vanity."[5] Saint Francis was so moved by the spirit of detachment he saw in Brother Juniper that on one occasion he cried out, "My brothers, if only I had a great forest of such junipers!"[6]

We need to hear their word today: we who love greed more than we love the gospel, we who live in fear, and not in trust. We need to hear their word today: we who define people in terms of their net worth, we who push and shove to gain an ever larger piece of the consumer pie.

The Puritan response to the issue of money is seen in their stress upon *industry*. The Puritans emphasized industry because they believed intensely in the sanctity of all honorable work. They completely rejected the ancient division between things sacred and things secular. For them, vocation was an expression of one's spiritual life. In *The Tradesman's Calling*, Richard Steele declared that it is in the shop "where you may most confidently expect the presence and blessing of God."[7]

Their vocation was a calling of God. Cotton Mather declared, "Oh, let every Christian walk with God, when he works at his calling, act in his occupation with an eye to God, act as under the eye of God."[8] Work was an opportunity to glorify God and to serve one's neighbor.

They also stressed moderation in work. They scorned the mentality of the workaholic as much as they did sloth. Since work was to honor God rather than to make money, too much work could be as evil as too little work. Richard Steele notes that a person should not "accumulate two or three callings merely to increase his riches."[9]

We need to hear their word today: we who find work meaningless and dull, we who are tempted by sloth and laziness. We need to hear their word today: we who are workaholics, we who take multiple jobs in order to move up the economic ladder.

We can be glad for the monastic vow of poverty and the Puritan "vow" of industry, but we today need a new "vow" that responds creatively and boldly to the money issue. It must be a vow that will reject the modern mania for wealth without a morbid asceticism. It must be a vow that calls us to use money without serving money. It must be a vow that brings money into obedience to the will and ways of God.

THE HISTORIC VOWS: SEX

People today are hopelessly confused about their sexuality. For vast numbers the word *love* means nothing more than a tumble in some bed. Many look upon an affair as a badge of honor. All the old foundations for permanence and fidelity seem to have eroded away. Bewildered by the modern confusion, many sincere people today struggle to define their own sexuality.

The vow of *chastity* was the monastic response to the issue of sex. They were saying far more than a negative word. They renounced marriage in order to learn vacancy. Chastity arose as a witness for a holy empty space in a world overcrowded with interpersonal relationships. Thomas Aquinas called celibacy a *vacare Deo*, "a vacancy for God." "To be a celibate," notes Henri Nouwen, "means to be empty for God, to be free and open for his presence, to be available for his service."[10]

The vow of chastity also witnesses against unrestrained self-indulgence. It reminds us that discipline and denial are gospel imperatives. You see, our sexual intoxication is only representative of an all-pervasive mood of intemperance that dominates the world in which we live today. The Franciscan Brother Giles once said, "By chastity I mean to keep guard over all the senses with the grace of God."[11] If we need anything today, it is to learn how "to keep guard over all the senses by the grace of God," and if the vow of chastity can remind us of this need, it has done us an immense service.

We need to hear their word today: we who are desperately afraid to be alone, we who try to replace God with interpersonal relationships. We need to hear their word today: we who are caught up in the modern mania of narcissism, we who avoid discipline as if it were a plague.

Faithfulness was the Puritan response to the issue of sex. Unfortunately the wholesomeness of their approach has been obscured for us by complete distortions of their thought. In fact, the misapprehension has gone so far that the word *Puritan* can function today as a noun defining someone plagued with sexual taboos and unhealthy inhibitions. Actually, that definition fits better the more squeamish nineteenth-century Victorians than the seventeenth- and eighteenth-century Puritans. No rigid ascetics, these were people who knew how to laugh and how to love. In 1660 Fritz-John Winthrop commissioned John Haynes to buy a pair of garters for Winthrop to present to his fiancée. In a letter enclosed with the garters Haynes teased Winthrop that "you would be glad to have a Lady leggs and all."[12] In a wedding sermon in 1694 John Cotton told the story of a couple who determined to live a contemplative life without sexual relations, and he assessed their decision as "blind zeal," noting that it was "not of that Holy Spirit which saith *It is not good that man should be alone*."[13]

They sought to think through to a serious Christian basis for marriage and family life. Perhaps their most radical departure from the Catholic-Anglican view was their conviction that companionship was the primary purpose of marriage and healthy sexuality within marriage was a vital part of this companionship. Francis Bremer has observed, "The stereotype of the Puritan as having been prudish and condemnatory about sex has no basis in fact. . . . As their diaries, letters, and other writings make evident, the Puritans were a good deal more comfortable discussing sexual matters than many of their descendants."[14]

They also labored to construct a Christian basis for divorce and remarriage. On this issue the Puritans were actually the liberals of their day. They rejected the medieval church's ban on divorce on both biblical and practical grounds. William Perkins advocated divorce for infidelity, desertion, disease, and insanity, with equal rights for men and women.* John Milton argued for incompatibility as valid grounds for divorce, since Puritan theology placed companionship as the primary purpose of marriage.[15]

We need to hear their word today: we who flit from marriage to marriage with the greatest of ease. We need to hear their word today: we who lay impossible burdens upon people in our frantic zeal to stem the tide of divorce.

We can appreciate the monastic vow of chastity and the Puritan "vow" of faithfulness, but we today urgently need a contemporary "vow" that responds forthrightly and compassionately to the sex issue. It must be a vow

* M. M. Knappen, *Tudor Puritanism: A Chapter in the History of Idealism* (Chicago: The University of Chicago Press, 1939), pp. 459–61. This chapter in Puritan history is really quite interesting and not without its controversies. An interesting sample of the debates that raged over this issue can be seen by reading John Rainolds, *A Defence of the Judgment of the Reformed Churches: That a Man May Lawfullie Not Only Put Awaie His Wife for Her Adulterie But Also Marrie Another* (1609) and the response of Edmund Bunry, *Of Divorce for Adulterie and Marring Again* (1610).

that will affirm our God-given sexuality without encouraging promiscuity. It must be a vow that gives wholeness to the marriage experience without depreciating the single life. It must be a vow that defines the moral parameters of our sexuality and also calls us to joyful expression within those parameters.

THE HISTORIC VOWS: POWER

The idolatry of today is the idolatry of power. Books by the score appeal to our Machiavellian passions. Today, by and large, political leaders give more energy to jockeying for position than to serving the public good; business executives care more for keeping on top of the heap than for producing a useful product; university professors seek sophistication more than truth; and religious leaders care more for their image than for the gospel. And in the midst of this power-crazed society many Christians wonder how to live with integrity.

The vow of *obedience* was the monastic response to the issue of power. They renounced power in order to learn service. Now, if the vows of poverty and chastity are incomprehensible to modern men and women, the vow of obedience is utterly reprehensible. The very idea of somebody—anybody—having any kind of say in our lives runs so counter to everything in our society that anger and even hostility is our almost automatic response.

The monastics, however, were trying to learn service through the vow of obedience. Obedience was an intense way of confessing their corporate life. They were accountable to each other and responsible for each other. Through obedience they sought to be receptive to the rightful rule of God through others. On one occasion Saint Francis asked Sister Clare and Brother Masseo to seek the mind of the Lord regarding his ministry. When they returned, Saint Francis knelt and said, "What does my Lord Jesus Christ order me to do?"[16] You see, he did not ask for their opinion or their counsel but for his marching orders. Under "holy obedience" he let go of his way in order to hear Christ's way, and on this occasion at least he learned to hear it through others.

Leonardo Boff put it well when he said, "Obedience is the greatest free decision one makes for God."[17] Perhaps the vow of obedience can help us see more fully that to lose ourselves is the only way to truly find ourselves.

We need to hear their word today: we who want to be accountable to no one, we who want to be responsible for no one. We need to hear their word today: we who lust for power and status, we who find serving others demeaning.

Order was the Puritan response to the issue of power. In the church order was built around their concept of "the Visible Covenant," which was a mutual commitment of support and accountability. The purpose of this mutual responsibility and care was to give "Church-power over one another mutually."[18] And when the purpose of this "Church-power" was to stir one another to love and good works, it helped immensely.

In government order was built around the idea of "the Holy Commonwealth." The vision was certainly ambitious: a government based upon the Bible with magistrates to execute the will of God. To their credit, the Puritans sought to use the power of the state to bring moral fiber to public as well as private life.*

We need to hear their word today: we who reject all

---

* The Puritan vision of order also had very negative consequences. When this "Church-power" was turned toward routing out heretics, as in the Salem witch trials, we see a Church-power gone sour. We can, of course, discover many of the same shortcomings in the monastic vows. Money, sex, and power are very seductive things, and even in religious garb, the temptations to manipulate and control, to suppress and oppress are very great.

order and all authority. We need to hear their word to-day: we who love our own way more than we love the divine fellowship.

Clearly the monastic vow of obedience and the Puritan "vow" of order can teach us many things, but the crying need today is for a new "vow" that responds creatively and positively to the issue of power. It must be a vow that is able to harness the good side of power without being obsessed by its shadow side. It must be a vow that will bring authority and submission into proper balance. It must be a vow that models leadership within the context of servanthood.

WHEN GOOD THINGS GO BAD

There is, of course, a proper place in Christian life and experience for money, sex, and power. When properly placed and effectively functioning, they have the ability as nothing else does to enhance and bless life. Money, for example, can enrich human life in wonderful ways. Food, shelter, education—these are things that money can help us acquire. More than once I have watched students literally jump for joy when a way has been found to finance their education. Or in the area of sex, I have counseled and prayed with young couples who have been wonderfully transformed by the inner healing of an old sexual hurt or by a new insight into their sexuality. Power can be used by individuals of genuine spiritual authority to bless and liberate virtually everyone around them. I have witnessed people whose very presence was enriching.

Again, when properly placed and effectively functioning, money, sex, and power have enormous ability to bring goodness into human life. Exactly what that place is and how they function there will be the enduring task of this book.

Having said this, however, we must also underscore

to ourselves again and again that we are dealing with explosive themes that easily turn into "demons" that make of our lives one great sorrow.

The demon in money is greed. Nothing can destroy human beings like the passion to possess. In *The Idiot*, Dostoevsky has one of his characters observe, "Every one is possessed with such a greed nowadays, they are all so overwhelmed by the idea of money that they seem to have gone mad."[19]

The demon in sex is lust. True sexuality leads to humanness, but lust leads to depersonalization. Lust captivates rather than emancipates, devours rather than nourishes.

The demon in power is pride. True power has as its aim to set people free, whereas pride is determined to dominate. True power enhances relationships; pride destroys them.

The demons of greed, lust, and pride can be exorcised, but let me warn you that the exorcisms will not come easily or quickly.* Hasty exorcisms almost always drive out angels as well as demons. And once the demons are gone, we had better be clear about what is to fill the vacancy, for empty spaces never remain empty for long (Matt. 12:43-45).

We must understand that these are not matters we can be neutral about and hope they will go away. If we fail to exorcise the demons of greed, lust, and pride, we are doomed to eventually be dominated by them. They may take on the appearance of angels, but they will be demonic powers nonetheless.

We may take money and use it to help people, but if it has within it the demon seed of greed, we will put people into our debt in ruinous ways. And when greed is tied to

---

* My reference here to "demons" and exorcism is purely metaphorical. I am *not* suggesting that anyone who evidences characteristics of greed or lust or pride is "possessed" and needs exorcism.

giving, it is particularly destructive because it appears so
good, so much like an angel of light. When we give out of
a spirit of greed, an all-pervasive attitude of paternalism
poisons the entire enterprise. When greed motivates our
giving, we are still trying to profit from the transaction.
That is why the apostle Paul says that we can give away
everything but if we lack love we "gain nothing" (1 Cor.
13:3).

When we turn to the sexual experience, we discover
that lust, too, can appear as an angel of light. Lust impris-
ons the other person, and yet the incarceration can look
good from many angles. It promises security and safety
from a hostile world. In fact, many people will enter a
marriage relationship based upon lust rather than love
simply because the two often look so much alike. But the
end result of lust is dehumanization, in which the important thing is not the person but the possession of that
person. People become things to acquire, prizes to win,
objects to control. "My wife" or "my husband" becomes
"my toy."

Or we may take power and use it in such good ways,
but if the demonic force of pride still resides, the end
result will be manipulation, domination, and tyranny.
The Jonestown tragedy is a blatant example. Here was an
enterprise that began as a noble ministry but ended in
destruction. Power infested with pride will surely give
rise to egomania.

A NEW CALL TO OBEDIENCE

How do we live faithfully today with regard to the
issues of money, sex, and power? This is *the* question that
demands an answer today. The answer will not come
quickly or easily; it will require our best thinking and our
greatest devotion.

The monastic movement, with its vows of poverty,

chastity, and obedience, was an attempt to answer this question within the context of one culture. The Puritan efforts to bring monastic conviction into common life through their concerns for industry, faithfulness, and order was an attempt to answer this question within the context of a quite different culture. The issue that we must now face is how to answer this question within the context of our own culture.

We can learn much from the many groups in the past who have sought to live obediently, but we cannot deal with the issues of money, sex, and power in precisely the same way they did. We live in another era. We face many problems that did not even exist for them. New situations demand new responses. And so we are faced with the necessity for framing a contemporary response to the issues of money, sex, and power.

Today we need a new articulation of Christian "vows." Such vows will constitute a new call to obedience to Christ in the midst of contemporary society. The need is great. The task is urgent. Our century longs for a new demonstration of joyful, confident, obedient living. May we be just such a demonstration.

PART I
Money

2. The Dark Side of Money

> Money has demonically usurped the role in modern society which the Holy Spirit is to have in the Church.
>
> —THOMAS MERTON

Martin Luther astutely observed, "There are three conversions necessary: the conversion of the heart, mind, and the purse."[1] Of these three, it may well be that we moderns find the conversion of the purse the most difficult. It is hard for us even to talk about money. In fact, I recently heard of a couple, both psychologists, who would speak openly and frankly in front of their children about sex, death, and all manner of difficult subjects, but would go into the bedroom and close the door when they wanted to talk about money. In a survey of psychotherapists in which they listed things they should not do with their patients, it was found that lending a client money was a greater taboo than touching, kissing, or even sexual intercourse. For us, money is indeed a forbidden subject.

And yet Jesus spoke about money more frequently than any other subject except the kingdom of God. He gave an unusual amount of time and energy to the money question. In the moving story about the "widow's mite," we are told that Jesus intentionally sat in front of the treasury and watched people putting in their offerings (Mark 12:41). By design, he saw what they gave and discerned the spirit in which they gave. For Jesus, giving was not a private matter. He did not—as we so often do today—glance away embarrassed at prying into someone's personal business. No, Jesus considered it public business and used the occasion to teach about sacrificial giving.

Jesus' careful attention to the money question is one of the truly amazing things about the Gospel narratives. The range of his concern is startling: from the parable of the sower to the parable of the rich farmer, from the encounter with the rich young ruler to the encounter with Zacchaeus, from teachings on trust in Matthew 6 to teachings on the dangers of wealth in Luke 6.

TWO STREAMS

In my book *Freedom of Simplicity* I went into detail about the biblical perspective on money in both Old and New Testaments; I will not retrace my steps here.* We do, however, need to be aware of the two major streams of teaching regarding money that we find in the New Testament and, indeed, throughout the Bible.

These two divergent streams of teaching are certainly paradoxical, and sometimes they seem downright contradictory. This should not surprise us. God so superintended the writing of the Scriptures that they accurately reflect the real world in which we live, and most of us are so well acquainted with paradox and perplexity in our own experience that we understand. Only the arrogant and the dogmatic find paradox hard to accept.

THE DARK SIDE

The first stream of teaching we find is what I have chosen to call the dark side of money. I am referring both to the way in which money can be a threat to our relation-

---

* See *Freedom of Simplicity* (San Francisco: Harper & Row, 1981). Note especially chapters 2 and 3. In that book I was dealing with the issue of Christian simplicity, which is a larger question than money, but you will find most of Jesus' teaching regarding money there. Also, I devote chapter 6 of *Celebration of Discipline* (San Francisco: Harper & Row, 1978) to that question.

ship with God and to the radical criticism of wealth that we find so much of in Jesus' words. The warnings and exhortations are repetitious, almost monotonous. "Woe to you that are rich" (Luke 6:24). "You cannot serve God and mammon" (Luke 16:13). "Do not lay up for yourselves treasures on earth" (Matt. 6:19). "It is easier for a camel to go through the eye of a needle than for a rich man to enter the kingdom of God" (Matt. 19:24). "Take heed, and beware of all covetousness" (Luke 12:15). "Sell your possessions, and give alms" (Luke 12:33). "Give to every one who begs from you; and of him who takes away your goods do not ask them again" (Luke 6:30). And, of course, many more statements could be added to this sample listing.

The point is that the teaching is very clear and very severe. Right at this juncture we face a real temptation to tone down the criticism immediately, or at least to try to balance it with more positive biblical statements. But this is the very thing we must not do, at least not yet. First we are obliged to allow Scripture to speak to us on this issue. We must not take the sting out of the teaching too quickly. Before we try to explain why it cannot apply to our day, before we insert a dozen qualifications, before we try to interpret or explain or resolve the problem in any way, we simply need to *hear* the word of Scripture.

The truth is that it is not really difficult to discover what the Bible teaches about money.* If we will simply read it through with honest hearts, we can come to a rather clear sense of the direction of Scripture on this subject. The Bible is much more clear and straightforward about money than it is about many other issues. Our difficulty is not in understanding the teaching; our

---

* I am well aware of the difficulties posed, for example, by the differing emphasis of Old and New Testament regarding money but those problems should not keep us from acknowledging the overall clarity of the biblical witness.

problem lies in another direction. The most difficult thing we have to deal with when we begin to look at the dark side of money is fear. If we have any sense at all, these words of Jesus really do frighten us. They frighten me. And we will not be able to hear the Scripture on this issue until we come to terms with our fear.

There is good reason for fear. These statements of Jesus fly in the face of virtually everything we have been taught about what constitutes an abundant life. Their implications are staggering for us, for the Church, and for the wider world of economics and politics. They challenge our privileged status in the world and call us to vigorous sacrificial action. There is indeed good reason for fear.

But the reason for fear is yet more complicated. We may fear being without money because our parents were without money. We may fear failure. We may fear success. Our parents may have had anxieties about money that we have made our own. We may have fears that stem from watching the absurdities to which some people have taken the teachings of Jesus.

I do not want to make light of these fears of ours in any way. Many of them are completely justified, and all of them need to be dealt with. In due time I will be discussing how we can come to terms with our fears. For now, it is enough to know that as the spirit of fear is replaced with the spirit of trust we will become more and more able to hear Jesus' radical criticism of wealth.

THE LIGHT SIDE

If we focused our attention exclusively on the warnings, we would have a distorted picture of the New Testament teaching. There is another stream of teaching that stresses what I have chosen to call the light side of money. I am referring to the way in which money can be used to enhance our relationship with God and bless humankind. A giving spirit can enhance the life of prayer and devotion. When Zacchaeus was freed to begin transferring his treasure from earth to heaven, Jesus joyfully announced, "Today salvation has come to this house" (Luke 19:9). The anointings of Jesus were each extravagant and each praised (Matt. 26:6–12; Luke 7:36–50; John 12:1–8). The good Samaritan used money generously and drew close to the kingdom of God.

The teaching on the light side goes further still. At times there seems to be a carefree, almost nonchalant attitude toward wealth. Jesus allowed well-to-do women to support his ministry (Luke 8:1–3). He ate with the rich and privileged (Luke 11:37; 14:1). He joined in the lavish wedding feast of Cana (John 2:1). The apostle Paul was as content with abounding as he was with being abased, as content with plenty as he was with hunger (Phil. 4:12). And this, of course, is only a sample of the teaching.

How do we resolve the apparent conflict between the dark side and the light side? My attempt to do so will come later, in chapter 4. Besides, an instant resolution is probably not desirable, for it would keep us from hearing Jesus' teaching about the dark side of money.

PREVAILING DISTORTIONS

Our desire to resolve the problem quickly—and our consequent failure to hear the dark side—has brought about two prevailing distortions. The first is that money is a sign of God's blessing, and hence poverty is a sign of God's displeasure. This has been turned into a religion of personal peace and prosperity: crudely stated, "Love Jesus and get rich." Many churches are saturated with readily available gimmicks for blessedness, all the way from exact mathematical formulas (God will bless you sevenfold) to much more subtle but equally destructive forms. The distortion, of course, rests upon a piece of important biblical teaching, namely, the great generosity of God. But it is a distortion because it turns one aspect of the Bible's teaching on money into the whole message. This distortion fails to hear money's dark side.

Even the disciples struggled with this distortion. Remember how astonished they were when Jesus declared that a camel could slip through the eye of a needle more easily than the wealthy could enter the kingdom of God. Their amazement was primarily due to their belief that the wealth of the rich young ruler was a sign of God's special favor upon him. No wonder they exclaimed, "Who then can be saved?" (Matt. 19:25). Or think of Job's comforters—their firm conviction that he must have sinned stemmed from the obvious fact of his economic misfortune. Repeatedly Jesus opposed this false and destructive doctrine, showing instead that in the economy of God the poor, the bruised, the broken were special objects of his blessing and concern (Matt. 5:1–12). He made it quite clear that wealth itself was no assurance of God's blessing (Luke 6:24).*

A second distortion about money is found in the prevailing view of stewardship today. Discussions of stewardship, almost without exception, view money as completely neutral and depersonalized. It is merely "a medium of exchange," as we say. God has given us money to use, to administer, to put into service, goes the teaching. And so the emphasis is always placed upon the best use, the proper stewardship, of the resources God has entrusted to us.

What all this talk about stewardship fails to see is that money is not just a neutral medium of exchange but a

---

* Donald Kraybill, in chapter seven of his book *The Upside Down Kingdom* (Scottdale, Penn.: Herald Press, 1978), discusses ten different attempts to evade Jesus' hard teachings on money. Nearly all ten stem from this fatal distortion of the biblical witness.

"power" with a life of its own. And very often it is a "power" that is demonic in character. As long as we think of money in impersonal terms alone, no moral problems exist aside from the proper use of it. But when we begin to take seriously the biblical perspective that money is animated and energized by "powers," then our relationship to money is filled with moral consequence.

MONEY AS A POWER

The New Testament teaching on money makes sense only when we see it in the context of the "principalities and powers." The good creation of God has both "visible" and "invisible" realities (Col. 1:16). To describe certain aspects of the invisible realities the apostle Paul uses such terms as "principalities," "powers," "thrones," "dominions," and "authorities."* Originally part of God's good creation, these powers have, because of sin, lost their proper relationship to God. They have fallen and are in revolt against their creator. This is why the powers bring with them such mixed results—good and evil, blessing and cursing. This is why Paul can speak of the powers (*exousia*) as both the stabilizing forces in the Roman government (Rom. 13:1) and the demonic forces we are to wage war against (Eph. 6:12). The conviction was that in back of earthly rulers, social institutions, and many other things were invisible spiritual authorities and powers that were of an angelic or demonic nature.

Money is one of these powers. When Jesus uses the Aramaic term *mammon* to refer to wealth, he is giving it a personal and spiritual character. When he declares, "You cannot serve God and mammon" (Matt. 6:24), he is personifying mammon as a rival god. In saying this, Jesus is

* See, e.g., Col. 1:16; 2:15; Rom. 8:38; 1 Cor. 15:24–26; Eph. 1:21; 2:2; 3:10; 6:12; etc.

making it unmistakably clear that money is not some impersonal medium of exchange. Money is not something that is morally neutral, a resource to be used in good or bad ways depending solely upon our attitude toward it. Mammon is a power that seeks to dominate us.

When the Bible refers to money as a power, it does not mean something vague or impersonal. Nor does it mean power in the sense we mean when we speak, for example, of "purchasing power." No, according to Jesus and all the writers of the New Testament, behind money are very real spiritual forces that energize it and give it a life of its own. Hence, money is an active agent; it is a law unto itself; and it is capable of inspiring devotion.

It is the ability of money to inspire devotion that brings its dark side to the forefront. Dietrich Bonhoeffer has rightly said, "Our hearts have room only for one all-embracing devotion, and we can only cleave to one Lord."[2] What we must recognize is the seductive power of mammon. Money has power, spiritual power, to win our hearts. Behind our coins and dollar bills or whatever material form we choose to give to our money are spiritual forces.

It is the spiritual reality behind money that we want so badly to deny. For years I felt that Jesus was exaggerating by fixing such a huge gulf between mammon and God. Couldn't we show how advanced we are in the Christian life by giving each his due, God and mammon? Why not be joyful children of the world just as we are joyful children of God? Aren't the goods of the earth meant for our happiness? But the thing I failed to see, and the thing that Jesus saw so clearly, is the way in which mammon makes a bid for our hearts. Mammon asks for our allegiance in a way that sucks the milk of human kindness out of our very being.

That is why so much of Jesus' teaching regarding wealth is evangelistic in character. He calls people to turn away from the mammon god in order to worship the one true God. When a would-be disciple told Jesus of his determination to follow him anywhere he went, Jesus responded, "Foxes have holes, and birds of the air have nests; but the Son of man has nowhere to lay his head" (Matt. 8:20).

The rich young ruler asked Jesus how he could have eternal life and received the startling reply, "Go, sell what you possess and give to the poor, and you will have treasure in heaven; and come, follow me" (Matt. 19:21). The instruction makes sense only when we see that the rich young ruler's wealth was a rival god seeking his complete devotion. And note that when this young man went away sorrowful Jesus did not run after him and suggest that he only meant it metaphorically, that all that was really required was a tithe. No, money had become an all-consuming idol, and it had to be rejected totally.

Jesus' lunch with Zacchaeus had a remarkable outcome. This chief tax collector, for whom money was everything, was so freed by the life and presence of Christ that he declared, "Half of my goods I give to the poor; and if I have defrauded any one of anything, I restore it fourfold" (Luke 19:8). But even more striking is Jesus' response, "Today salvation has come to this house" (Luke 19:9).

Do you see what an utter contrast this is to the normal means of evangelism today? Our method is to get them "saved," and then later on instruct them in "Christian stewardship." For us, salvation usually consists in assenting to three or four statements and saying the prescribed prayer. But Jesus warns people to count the cost of discipleship before they ever enter into it. Not to do so would be as foolish as a construction company starting a skyscraper without calculating the expense, or a military dictator beginning a war without assessing his chances of winning (Luke 14:25–32). Jesus concludes this sobering teaching with such disturbing words that we find it hard to believe he could possibly mean what he says: "So therefore, whoever of you does not renounce all that he has cannot be my disciple" (Luke 14:33). I have yet to go to an evangelistic meeting and hear that kind of statement made before the invitation is given. But that is exactly what Jesus did, not just once but repeatedly.

For Christ money is an idolatry we must be converted *from* in order to be converted *to* him. The rejection of the god mammon is a necessary precondition to becoming a disciple of Jesus. And in point of fact, money has many of the characteristics of deity. It gives us security, can induce guilt, gives us freedom, gives us power and seems to be omnipresent. Most sinister of all, however, is its bid for omnipotence.

It is money's desire for omnipotence, for all power, that seems so strange, so out of place. It seems that money is not willing to rest contented in its proper place alongside other things we value. No, it must have supremacy. It must crowd out all else: This is, I say, the strange thing about money. We attach importance to it far beyond its worth. In fact, we attach ultimate importance to it. It is tremendously instructive to stand back and observe the frantic scramble of people for money. And this does not occur just among the poor and starving. Quite to the contrary—the super-wealthy, who have really nothing to gain by more money, still seek it furiously. The middle class, who are really quite adequately cared for (and who are from a global perspective the wealthy), continue to buy more houses than they need, to acquire more cars than they need, to have more clothes than they need. Many of us could live on half what we now receive without much serious sacrifice, yet we feel we are just barely making ends meet—and we feel this way whether we are earning $15,000 or $50,000 or $150,000.

Think of the symbols we attach to money—symbols

that are unrelated to its true value. If money were only a medium of exchange, it would make no sense at all to attach prestige to it, for example. And yet we do. We value people in relation to their income; we give people status and honor in relation to how much money they have. We dare to ask that question of questions that always reveals far more about ourselves than about the other person, "How much is he (or she) worth?" Dr. Lee Salk, a professor of psychology at the New York Hospital Cornell Medical Center, declared, "People jockey to find out what other people earn because, in our society, money is a symbol of strength, influence and power."[3]

In this century we have witnessed some of the most massive efforts in history to break the power of money through political means, but they have all failed. Both China and Cuba, for example, got rid of money as a means of exchange and then made it impossible to save money, to build up capital. But in time these imperatives had to be abandoned, and first money as a means of exchange, then money as a means of savings, reappeared. Finally, cash production bonuses were reinstated. Now, I give this example, not as a criticism of communist regimes, but as an example of what Jacques Ellul calls "the incredible power of money, which survives every trial, every upset, as if a merchant mentality has so permeated the world's consciousness that there is no longer any possibility of going against it."[4]

These strange facts make sense only as we come to understand the spiritual reality of money. Behind money are invisible spiritual powers, powers that are seductive and deceptive, powers that demand an all-embracing devotion. It is this fact that the apostle Paul saw when he observed that "the love of money is the root of all evils" (1 Tim. 6:10). Many have rightly observed that Paul did not say "money" but "the love of money." Given the almost universal love of money, however, they are often the same in practice.

Paul saw the same thing Jesus was dealing with in his many statements about money, namely, that it is a god that is out to gain our allegiance. By saying that the love of money is the root of all evils he does not mean in a literal sense that money produces all evils. He means that there is no kind of evil the person who loves money will not do to get it and hold onto it. All restraint is removed; the lover of money will do anything for it. And that is precisely its seductive character; for the person who loves money, no half measures will do. The person is hooked. Money becomes a consuming, life-dominating problem. It is a god demanding an all-inclusive allegiance.

This is why Jesus' cleansing of the temple was so pivotal. It was a deliberate act to symbolize that in the coming of the Messiah the religion of Israel was to be purged of its mammon worship. We must remember that the temple trade was good business in many ways. A valuable service was being provided, and although the prices were inflated, it was no more than what the market would bear. But Jesus saw through all that to the idolatry, the threat to the worship of the one true God.

As we come to understand better the dark side of money—its demonic tendency—we have a greater appreciation of Jesus' radical criticism of wealth. Without this insight it would be very easy for us to make Jesus' critical statements regarding money apply only to the dishonest rich. Certainly those who have obtained their money honestly and use it wisely are not included in his criticism—are they? But much of Jesus' teaching cannot be confined to the dishonest wealthy, for it speaks with equal severity to those who have acquired their wealth justly. There is every indication that the rich young ruler had gained his wealth honestly (Luke 18:18–30). In the story of the rich man and Lazarus there is no hint of dishonesty related to the condemnation of the rich man (Luke 16:19–31). In the parable of the rich farmer who tore down his barns to make way for expansion, we have every indication of honesty and industry (Luke 12:16–21). We would call him prudent—Jesus called him a fool.

This radical criticism of wealth makes no sense to us at all unless we see it in the context of its spiritual reality. It is one of the principalities and powers that must be conquered and redeemed through the blood of Jesus Christ *before* it can be usable for the greater good of the kingdom of God.

CONQUERING THE DARK SIDE

How is the god mammon conquered? Do we embrace it and try to use it for good purposes? Do we flee from it in total renunciation and divestiture?

Part of the reason these are difficult questions to answer is that the Bible does not offer us a Christian doctrine of money. It is a misuse and abuse of the Bible to make it yield some economic theory or give us ten rules for financial rectitude. But what it does offer us is even better: a perspective from which to view all life's economic decisions and a promise of dialogue, personal counseling in all life's financial decisions. The Holy Spirit is with us; Jesus is our present Teacher, and he will guide us through the money maze in all its personal and social complexity.

With that understanding, I would like to share several practical suggestions, knowing that they must be sifted through the filter of your own unique personality and circumstances. Perhaps they can serve in some way as signposts to encourage you in your journey.

First, let us get in touch with our *feelings* about money. For most of us the biggest obstacle to overcome is not that of understanding what the Bible teaches about money but that of coming to terms with our fear, insecurity, and guilt about money. We really are threatened by the subject of money. We are afraid that we have too little, and we are afraid that we have too much. And our fears are often irrational. For example, people who earn twenty times the average income of a citizen of Kenya are afraid of being on the brink of starvation. Or some of us are terrified of the possibility that others might overestimate our wealth and conclude that we are greedy.

These feelings are real and need to be taken seriously. Often they stem from childhood memories. I remember as a child having one ability that gave me unusual "wealth"; I could play marbles better than any other kid in the school. Since we always played for "keeps," I could often wipe out another boy's fortune before the noon recess was over. On one occasion I remember taking a huge sack of marbles, throwing them one by one into a muddy drainage ditch, and watching with delight as the other boys scrambled to find them. Through that single experience I began to sense something of the power wealth can give and the manipulative ends to which it can be put.

Some of us grew up during the depression years and know firsthand the pervasive anxiety of scarcity. Because of that experience, a holding, hoarding spirit is almost instinctive in us, and the very idea of letting go of a possession is frightening. Others of us grew up in an era of affluence and are keenly aware of the spiritual dangers of too much; the notions of conserving and being frugal feel like vices rather than virtues. It is only as we come to terms with these and the many other feelings that have shaped our understanding of money that we can act upon the biblical call to faithfulness.

Second, by a conscious act of the will, let us stop denying our wealth. Let us look at the large picture. Rather than comparing ourselves to others like ourselves, so that we can always claim comparative poverty, let us become world citizens, looking at ourselves in relation to all humanity.

Those who own a car are among the world's upper class. Those who own a home are more wealthy than 95 percent of all the people on this planet. The very fact that you were able to purchase this book probably puts you among the world's wealthy. The very fact that I had the time to write this book puts me in the same category. Let us get away from our pervasive dishonesty and frankly admit our wealth. Although most of us have a difficult time balancing our budgets, we must recognize that as world citizens we are among the very wealthy.

But please note that this is not intended to make us feel guilty; it is intended to help us capture an accurate picture of the real situation in the world. We are wealthy. The very fact that we have the leisure time to read a book or watch television means that we are wealthy. We do not need to be ashamed of our wealth or try to hide it from ourselves and others. It is only as we admit our wealth and quit trying to run from it that we are in a position to conquer it and use it for God's good purposes.

Third, let us create an atmosphere in which confession is possible. Much of our preaching on money has been either to condemn it or praise it but not to help each other relate to it. Many of us feel isolated and alone, as if we were the only ones who count our gold in the night. How much better it would be to create a climate of acceptance in which we can talk about our mutual problems and frustrations, confess our fears and temptations. We can listen with empathy to the confession of someone who has been seduced by sex; let us just as freely hear the confession of someone who has been seduced by money. Let us learn to receive from each other the heart cry, "Forgive me, for I have sinned; money has captured my heart!"

We need others who will hear our fear and hurt, accepting it and lifting it on our behalf into the arms of God. For the Church to function as the Church, it needs to create an environment in which our failures over money can come to the surface and we can be healed.

Fourth, let us discover one other person who will struggle with us through the money maze. If it could be our husband or wife, that, I think, would be ideal. Together we covenant to help each other detect when the seductive power of money is beginning to win. This needs to be done in a spirit of love and graciousness, but it does need to be done. Anything that is made totally private and is never open to public correction will be distorted. All of us need as much help as possible to unearth our blind spots. Perhaps we want more things than are good for us—we need someone to help us face that fact. Perhaps we need to venture forth courageously into the business world for Christ and his kingdom—we need those who will encourage us in this ministry. Perhaps a spirit of greed has crept into our business dealings—we need people who will help us see it. Perhaps our fears keep us from the joyful life of trust—we need those who will prod us into faith.

Fifth, let us discover ways to get in touch with the poor. One of the most damaging things affluence does is allow us to distance ourselves from the poor so we no longer see their pain. We then can create an illusionary world that prevents us from evaluating life in the light of "love of neighbor."

What can we do? We can make a conscious choice to be among the poor, not to preach to them but to learn from them. We can read books, like *The Grapes of Wrath* and *Songs from the Slums*, that capture the smell and texture of life on the other side. We can stop watching the television programs that concentrate exclusively on the plastic world of the affluent. (If we do watch them, we can do so with discernment, knowing that it is a dream world that can easily insulate us from the pain and suffering and agony of the vast majority of humanity.)

Sixth, let us experience the meaning of inner renunciation. Abraham was asked to sacrifice his son, Isaac. And I can well imagine that by the time he came down from the mountain, the words *my* and *mine* had forever changed their meaning for him. The apostle Paul speaks of "having nothing, and yet possessing everything" (2 Cor. 6:10). As we enter the school of inner renunciation we come into that state in which nothing belongs to us and yet everything is available to us.

We badly need a conversion in our understanding of ownership. Perhaps we need to stamp everything in our possession with the reminder "Given by God, owned by God, and to be used for the purposes of God." We need to find ways to remind ourselves over and over again that the earth is the Lord's, not ours.

Seventh, let us give with glad and generous hearts. Giving has a way of routing out the tough old miser within us. Even the poor need to know that they can give. Just the very act of letting go of money, or some other treasure, does something within us. It destroys the demon greed.

Some will be led, like Saint Francis of Assisi, to give away everything and embrace "Lady Poverty." That is not a command for all, but it is the word of the Lord for some, as Jesus' encounter with the rich young ruler testifies. We must not despise people called to this form of giving but rejoice with them in their growing freedom from the god mammon.

The rest of us can find other ways to give. We can find needy people who have no way to repay us and give to them. We can give to the Church. We can give to educational institutions. We can give to missions. We can take the money we want to give and throw a high holy party for those who need to celebrate: the idea has good biblical precedent (Deut. 14:22–27). But whatever we do, let us give, give, give. Gordon Cosby has noted that "to give away money is to win a victory over the dark powers that oppress us."[5]

Perhaps you have found this a difficult chapter to read; I found it a difficult one to write. I so much wanted to get on to the good, the positive, the light side of money! We all like the affirmative viewpoint, so it is natural to downplay the negative, critical aspects. And yet, we really need to come to terms with the indisputable fact that, by far, most of Jesus' statements regarding money are about the dark side. And now we understand why this is so: only until we have faced and conquered the hellish character of money are we candidates for receiving and using its beneficial side. We now turn our attention to the light side of money.

3.   The Light Side of Money

The only right stewardship is that which is tested by the rule of love.

—JOHN CALVIN

The issue of money would be much easier to deal with if it were all bad. Our task then would be to denounce it and withdraw from it. That, however, is the one thing we cannot do if we want to be faithful to the biblical witness. Though the Bible gives repeated warnings about the dark side of money, it also contains a stream of teaching on the light side of money. In this tradition, money is seen as a blessing from God and, even more startling, as a means of enhancing our relationship with God.

THE OLD TESTAMENT WITNESS

The Old Testament bears repeated witness to this reality. In the creation story we are struck by the refrain that this world that God created is good. The garden of Eden was a lavish provision for the original pair.

God's great generosity can be seen in his care for Abraham. God said that he would make Abraham's name great and prosper him. And he kept his word, for we read that "Abram was very rich in cattle, in silver, and in gold" (Gen. 13:2). Isaac was blessed in a similar fashion, so much so that we are told that because of his great wealth "the Philistines envied him" (Gen. 26:14).

We are told that Job was a man of great wealth and that he was "blameless and upright, one who feared God, and turned away from evil" (Job 1:1). After his trial by fire, God restored Job's fortunes twofold (Job 42:10).

Solomon's great wealth was not viewed as something to be embarrassed about; rather, it was considered as evidence of God's favor (1 Kings 3:13). The Bible gives considerable space to cataloging Solomon's riches and then concludes, "Thus King Solomon excelled all the kings of the earth in riches and in wisdom" (1 Kings 10:23). The famous pilgrimage of the queen of Sheba to the court of Solomon underscores his prosperity. The queen exclaims, "I did not believe the reports until I came and my own eyes had seen it; and, behold, the half was not told me; your wisdom and prosperity surpass the report which I heard" (1 Kings 10:7).

The list could go on for some time, from the promise of a land flowing with milk and honey to the promise of the windows of heaven opening to pour out a material blessing beyond what we could contain (Mal. 3:10). Material things are neither antithetical nor inconsequential to the spiritual life but intimately and positively related to it.

THE NEW TESTAMENT WITNESS

Nor is the New Testament devoid of this emphasis. Money is often seen as a way of enhancing our relationship with God and expressing our love for our neighbor. The wise men brought their wealth to the Christ child as a means of worship. Zacchaeus gave generously, and the poor widow gave sacrifically. Wealthy women helped support the band of disciples (Luke 8:2-3). Both Joseph of Arimathea and Nicodemus used their wealth in the service of Christ (Matt. 27:57-61; John 19:38-42).

By teaching us to pray for daily bread, Jesus brought the concern for material provision into intimate relationship with the spiritual life. Material things are not to be despised or thought of as something outside the parame-

ters of true spirituality. Indeed, material provisions are
the lavish gifts of a bountiful God.

In Acts we are told of Barnabas, who was a true son of
encouragement when he used his land investments to aid
the early church (Acts 4:36-37). We are given the wonderful story of Cornelius, who "gave alms liberally to the
people, and prayed constantly to God" (Acts 10:2). We
are reminded of Lydia, the seller of purple, who used her
status and resources to benefit the early church (Acts 16:
14).

The apostle Paul uses the collection for the saints in
Jerusalem as an opportunity to teach the spiritual benefits
of cheerful giving (2 Cor. 8 and 9). He even lists giving as
one of the spiritual gifts (Rom. 12:8).

From this brief overview it is clear that the New Testament contains a stream of teaching that views money in a
positive way. Let us now focus our attention on how
money can enhance our relationship with God.

THE GOOD EARTH

Throughout Scripture the provision of those things
necessary to carry on human life adequately is seen as the
gracious gift of a loving God. Everything that God created
is good, very good. It is meant to bless and enhance human life. How thankful we can be for these bountiful
signs of God's goodness! As I write these words, the
birds outside are singing, perhaps in thanksgiving for the
bounty and beauty of sky and sea and land. We can join
with them in cheerful song, for God has indeed given us
a good world to enjoy. The very bounty of the earth can
draw us closer to God in thanksgiving and praise.

Most wonderful of all is how so much of what comes is
not the result of our doing but a gift, unearned and
unearnable. God told the children of Israel that he was
going to give them "great and goodly cities, which you

did not build, and houses full of all good things, which
you did not fill, and cisterns hewn out, which you did not
hew, and vineyards and olive trees, which you did not
plant" (Deut. 6:10b-11). Cities they did not build, wells
they did not dig, orchards they did not plant—this is
God's way with his people.

We do not need to look very deeply into our own
experience to know that this is so. Many times all our
hard work and clever scheming yield little or nothing,
and then all of a sudden we are flooded with good things
from completely unexpected sources. Many factors in our
business and economic lives are completely beyond our
control.

The farmers of ancient Israel had a keen sense of this
reality. They worked, to be sure, but they also knew that
they were helpless to grow grain. Drought, fire, pesti-
lence, and a hundred other things could wipe them out in
an instant. They knew and understood on a very deep
level that a good harvest was the gracious provision of a
loving God.

This is, of course, nothing more than the confession
that we live by grace. Though it is a wonderful truth to
know that we are saved by grace, it is equally wonderful
to know that we live by it as well. Though we labor, just
as the birds of the air labor, we do not need to grasp and
grab frantically, because we have One who cares for us
just as he cares for the birds of the air.

And so, as we learn to receive money and the things it
buys as gracious gifts from a loving God, we discover
how they enrich our relationship with God. Our experience resonates with the words of Deuteronomy, "God
will bless you in all your produce and in all the work of
your hands, so that you will be altogether joyful" (Deut.
16:15). Doxology becomes the posture of our experience.
Joy, thanksgiving, celebration—these mark our lives. One
reason so many of the ancient Jewish worship festivals

revolved around thanksgiving was because of their experience of the gracious provision of God.

GOD'S OWNERSHIP

Closely tied to God's provision is God's ownership. There is hardly anything more clear in the Bible than God's absolute right to property. To Job, God declares, "Whatever is under the whole heaven is mine" (Job 41: 11). To Moses, he says, "All the earth is mine" (Exod. 19:5-6). And the psalmist confesses, "The earth is the LORD's and the fulness thereof" (Ps. 24:1).

We moderns find it difficult to identify with this teaching. Much of our training draws from the Roman view that ownership is a "natural right." Hence the very idea that anything or anyone can infringe upon our "property rights" feels alien to our world view. This, coupled with our seemingly innate self-centeredness, means that, for us, "property rights" tend to take precedence over "human rights."

In the Bible, however, God's absolute rights as owner and our relative rights as stewards are unmistakably clear. As absolute owner, God put limits on the individual's ability to accumulate land or wealth. For example, a percentage of the produce of the land was to be given to the poor (Deut. 14:28-29). Every seventh year the land was to lie fallow, and whatever volunteer grain came up was for the needy, so that "the poor of your people may eat" (Exod. 23:11). Every fiftieth year was to be a Jubilee year, in which all slaves were to be set free, all debts were to be canceled, and all land was to return to its original owner. God's rationale for so violently upsetting everyone's economic applecarts was—very simply—that "the land is mine" (Lev. 25:23).

God's ownership of all things actually enhances our relationship with him. When we know—truly know—

that the earth is the Lord's, then property itself makes us more aware of God. For example, if we were staying in and caring for the vacation home of a famous actress, we would be reminded of her daily by the very fact of living in her home. A thousand things would bring her presence to mind. So it is in our relationship with God. The house we live in is his house, the car we drive is his car, the garden we plant is his garden. We are only temporary stewards of things that belong to Another.

Being aware of God's ownership can free us from a possessive and anxious spirit. After we have done what we can to care for those things that have been entrusted to us, we know that they are in bigger hands than ours. When John Wesley heard that his home had been destroyed by fire, he exclaimed, "The Lord's house burned. One less responsibility for me!"[1]

God's ownership of everything also changes the kind of question we ask in giving. Rather than, "How much of my money should I give to God?" we learn to ask, "How much of God's money should I keep for myself?" The difference between these two questions is of monumental proportions.

THE GRACE OF GIVING

The grace of giving is often a tremendous stimulant to the life of faith. This is why the offering is correctly placed as part of the worship experience.

In Isaiah 58 we read of a very religious people whose pious devotion counted for nothing because it was not matched with active caring for the poor and the oppressed. "Is not this the fast that I choose," proclaims God, "to loose the bonds of wickedness, to undo the thongs of the yoke, to let the oppressed go free, and to break every yoke?" (Isa. 58:6). Religious piety is bankrupt without justice. If you want your fasting to have true spiritual content, then you are to "share your bread with the hungry, and bring the homeless poor into your house" (Isa. 58:7).

If our spiritual vitality seems low, if Bible study produces only dusty words, if prayer seems hollow and empty, then perhaps a prescription of lavish and joyful giving is just what we need. Giving brings authenticity and vitality to our devotional experience.

Money is an effective way of showing our love to God because it is so much a part of us. One economist put it this way: "Money as a form of power is so intimately related to the possessor that one cannot consistently give money without giving self."[2] In a sense, money is coined personality, so tied to who we are that when we give it we are giving ourselves. We sing, "Take my life and let it be, consecrated, Lord, to Thee." But we must flesh out that consecration in specific ways, which is why the next line of the hymn says, "Take my silver and my gold, not a mite would I withhold." We consecrate ourselves by consecrating our money.

Dr. Karl Menninger once asked one wealthy patient, "What on earth are you going to do with all that money?" The patient replied, "Just worry about it, I suppose!" Dr. Menninger went on, "Well, do you get that much pleasure out of worrying about it?" "No," responded the patient, "but I get such terror when I think of giving some of it to somebody."[3]

Now, this "terror" is real. When we let go of money we are letting go of part of ourselves and part of our security. But this is precisely why it is important to do it. It is one way to obey Jesus' command to deny ourselves. "If any man would come after me, let him deny himself and take up his cross daily and follow me" (Luke 9:23).

When we give money we are releasing a little more of our egocentric selves and a little more of our false security. John Wesley declared that "if you have any desire to

escape the damnation of hell, give all you can; otherwise
I can have no more hope of your salvation than that of
Judas Iscariot."[4]

Giving frees us from the tyranny of money. But we do
not just give money; we give the things money has pur-
chased. In Acts the early Christian community gave
houses and land to provide funds for those in need (Acts
4:32-37). Have you ever considered selling a car or a
stamp collection to help finance someone's education?
Money has also given us the time and leisure to acquire
skills. What about giving those skills away? Doctors, den-
tists, lawyers, computer experts, and many others can
give their skills for the good of the community.

Giving frees us to care. It produces an air of expec-
tancy as we anticipate what God will lead us to give. It
makes life with God an adventure of discovery. We are
being used to help make a difference in the world, and
that is worth living for and giving for.[5]

CONTROLLING AND USING

Although giving must have a large place in Christian
experience, the control and use of money must have an
even larger place.[6] Believers who are rightly taught and
disciplined are enabled to hold possessions without corruption and use them for the greater purposes of the kingdom of God.

The truth is that total divestiture is usually a very poor
way to help the poor. Certainly it is vastly inferior to the
proper management and use of resources. How much
better to have wealth and resources in the hands of those
who are properly disciplined and informed by a Christian
world view than to abandon these things to the servants
of mammon!

Abraham managed large holdings for the glory of God
and the greater public good. So did Job and David and

Solomon. In the New Testament Nicodemus used both his wealth and his high position for the good of the Christian fellowship (John 7:50; 19:39). Because Barnabas had done well in managing his property holdings, he was able to help the early church when the need was acute (Acts 4:36–37).

Jesus gave us the parable of the talents (Matt. 25:14-30). Think of it: Jesus, who had spoken so severely of the danger of riches, now compares the kingdom of God to a man who entrusts his wealth to servants, fully expecting them to use it to make a profit. A talent was worth about a thousand dollars, and the man who had been given five thousand doubled his investment, as did the man with two thousand. But the poor fellow who had been given only one thousand was so afraid of losing it in the rough and tumble of the marketplace that he did nothing, and gained nothing. Jesus' words to this over-conservative servant are harsh indeed, "You wicked and slothful servant! You knew that I reap where I have not sowed, and gather where I have not winnowed? Then you ought to have invested my money with the bankers, and at my coming I should have received what was my own with interest. So take the talent from him, and give it to him who has the ten talents" (Matt. 25:26-28).

Now, it is not wrong to make spiritual applications of this parable, but it is wrong to completely divorce it from its economic context. Christians are to immerse themselves in the world of capital and business. That is a high and holy calling. It is a good thing for those under the rule of God to make money. We should not hide from these opportunities to labor for the sake of the kingdom of God.

Believers can and should be called into positions of power, wealth, and influence. It is a spiritual calling to take leadership roles in government, education, and business. Some are called to make money—lots of money

—for the glory of God and the larger public good. Others are called into positions of immense power and responsibility for the same purpose. Banks, department stores, factories, schools, and a thousand other institutions need the influence of Christian compassion and perspective.

But as I noted earlier, all this must be done in the context of a people who are "rightly taught and disciplined." You see, we need instruction on how to possess money without *being* possessed *by* money. We need help to learn how to own things without treasuring them. We need the disciplines that will allow us to live simply while managing great wealth and power.

The apostle Paul said that he had learned to be abased and that he had learned to abound; he could live in abundance, or in want, because "I can do all things through Christ who strengthens me" (Phil. 4:13, NKJV). It takes as much grace to abound as it does to be abased. If God chooses to bring us into great wealth or power, we are to humbly confess, "I can do all things through Christ who strengthens me," just as we do if severity and deprivation come.

The call of God is upon us to use money within the confines of a properly disciplined spiritual life and to manage money for the good of all humanity and for the glory of God. And when this is done we are drawn deeper into the divine Center. We stand amazed that God would use our meager efforts to do his work upon the earth. Resources are channeled into life-giving ministry. The helpless are helped. Projects that advance Christ's kingdom are financed. Great good is accomplished. Money is a blessing when it is used within the context of the life and power of God.

We can control and use money while we are alive: we can also control and use money at our death. A compassionate will is a good thing; it gives joy to know that our wealth will bless many after our death.

THE LESSONS OF TRUST

Another example of the light side of money is the way it can be used by God to build trust. When Jesus teaches us to pray for daily bread he is teaching us to live in trust. Huge stockpiles and elaborate backup systems are not necessary, because we have a heavenly Father who cares for us. When the children of Israel gathered manna in the wilderness they were allowed only a daily supply. Any more than the daily allotment would spoil. They were learning to live in trust, daily trust, upon Yahweh.

In giving these examples I am not speaking against retirement plans or savings accounts. What I am stressing is the way in which money can be used by God to build a spirit of trust within us.

During my senior year in high school I was invited to go on a summer mission venture among the Eskimo people of northern Alaska. Over the months I grew in my conviction that this was God's will for my life, yet I had no funds to make it a reality. Both my parents were seriously and chronically ill, and all the family's money had gone to pay medical bills.

In April I went on a weekend retreat with the other team members to make further plans for the trip. Over the weekend my conviction that I should go grew even stronger—but how? On my return home I discovered a letter in the mail with a thirty-dollar check. The letter was from someone who knew nothing of my summer hopes, but the note read simply, "For your expenses this summer." I took this check as God's gracious confirmation that I should go. I followed George Mueller's principle of telling no one my need except God, and it was a beautiful experience to watch over the ensuing months God's provision for every need for the trip. That was very faith-building for me as a young teenager.

But the story does not end there. When I returned

home my hopes for college were dim. All the money I had painstakingly saved through high school had gone for hospital care for my parents. Now the summer had been used, not to earn money, but to minister among the Eskimo people. A bit sad but still confident I had made the right decision, I applied for and was offered a job working for an insurance company. But before I could begin work, a series of events occurred that I could never have anticipated and for which I never had asked.

On Sunday, one week before fall college classes were to begin, I spoke in my home church on the experiences of the summer. After the service a couple in the congregation took me to their home for lunch and during the course of the afternoon inquired into my college plans. Within a few days this couple had formed a support group that helped me financially through four years of college and three years of graduate school. God had taken people and their sanctified use of money to teach me trust. And as is characteristic of the ways of God, it was above all I could ask or think.

That was my first experience in learning to trust God with money matters. Since that time, he has graciously used money to teach me more about trust and faith. You, I am sure, could relate similar experiences. Think of it, God takes so ordinary a thing as money, the very thing that so often rears its ugly head as a rival deity, and uses it to lead us forward in the kingdom of Christ.

PRACTICING THE LIGHT SIDE

We celebrate the light side of money by learning to cultivate a spirit of thanksgiving. I say "learn to cultivate" because it seems that thanksgiving does not come naturally to human beings. (Anyone who has children needs no further elaboration on that point.) However, we do need ways to help each other grow in gratitude. Often we miss the lavish provision of God—the air, the sunshine, the rain, the magnificent colors that delight our eyes, the many friendships that enrich our lives. The very rhythms of the earth are gracious gifts from the hand of the Creator.

Can we learn to wake up in the morning rejoicing in the miracle of sleep? Anyone who suffers from insomnia knows what a great gift sleep is. Perhaps at night we could go to the rooms of our sleeping children and sit down and watch them, all the time giving thanks. We can also look at our possessions and, without treasuring them, give thanks for them.

When we have a spirit of thanksgiving we can hold all things lightly. We receive; we do not grab. And when it is time to let go, we do so freely. We are not owners, only stewards. Our lives do not consist of the things that we have, for we live and move and breathe in God, not things. And may I add that this includes those intangible "things" that are often our greatest treasures—status, reputation, position. These are things that come and go in life, and we can learn to be thankful when they come and thankful when they go.

Perhaps we could discover new wineskins that would incarnate the Old Testament notion of the thank offering. Few of us are farmers, so fall harvest festivals are not as meaningful for us as they were for ancient Israel. But perhaps we can discover corresponding events that mark our economic lives. Maybe some payday we should convert our entire paycheck into dollar bills and then spread the money out on the living room floor just to help us visualize all that God has given us. We could then take what we plan to give away and actually give it in dollar bills, making the act visual to us in the way that grain was visual to the ancient Israelite making a thank offering.

Perhaps we could establish a Christian thanksgiving celebration for the signing of significant contracts. Maybe we could establish a consecration service for those called into the world of business. Whatever the ideas, the key is to continually discover a deeper, richer life of thanksgiving.

So far, we have sought to understand the two major streams of teaching in the Bible regarding money: the dark side and the light side. What we have not done yet is to merge the two streams together and show how they function in a working harmony in contemporary life. It is now time to attempt such a merger.

4. Kingdom Use of Unrighteous Mammon

Gain all you can, save all you can, give all you can.
—JOHN WESLEY

To my knowledge no one has attempted to reconcile Jesus' statement that we cannot serve God and mammon (Matt. 6:24) with his concern that we are to make friends by means of "unrighteous mammon" (Luke 16:9). This reconciliation, however, is precisely what is necessary if we are to rightly understand the Bible's witness to both the dark and the light side of money.

LUKE 16

In the opening verses of chapter 16 of Luke, Jesus tells a parable that has tied commentators into knots and puzzled ordinary Christians for centuries (Luke 16:1-13). And well it should, for the story is indeed an unusual one. However, it contains tremendous significance for our present study and holds the key to unlocking our understanding of both sides of money.

The parable itself is simple enough. A wealthy man discovers that his steward or business manager has been mishandling his funds and promptly fires him. But before his termination becomes final, the steward devises an ingenious plan to ensure his future. He calls in his employer's creditors, and one by one he writes off 20 to 50 percent of their debts. These people will thus be so indebted to him that when he is out of a job they will feel obliged to help him out.

The plan is obviously clever and just as obviously dishonest. When the master finds out what his steward has done, rather than throw him into prison as we might expect, he is so impressed by the man's ingenuity that he commends him on his prudence.

One reason we find this passage difficult is that Jesus uses what is so clearly a dishonest act to teach an important spiritual truth. However, Christ never commends the steward's dishonesty. Rather, he highlights his shrewdness in using economic resources for noneconomic goals —that is, using money to make friends so that when he needed it he would have a place to go.

Our biggest difficulty is with Jesus' own comments following the parable. He first notes that "the sons of this world are wiser in their own generation than the sons of light" (Luke 16:8). Next, he makes a most startling statement: "And I tell you, make friends for yourselves by means of unrighteous mammon, so that when it fails they may receive you into the eternal habitations" (Luke 16:9). In short, Jesus is telling us to use money in such a way that when it fails—and it will fail—we are still cared for.

Two things shock us in these words of Jesus: first, that mammon is unrighteous, and second, that we are to use it to make friends. The two ideas seem so opposed to each other that we find it hard to believe that Jesus could have meant them both.* The language, however, is clear enough—he did indeed mean to say that mammon is unrighteous *and* that we are to make friends with it.

---

* I am well aware of the various attempts to explain away the idea that mammon is unrighteous. The most argued position recently is that Jesus was using the term *unrighteous mammon* to refer to the practice of charging interest, which was prohibited to Jews and hence "unrighteous." Those who take this position include Dan Otto Via, Jr., in *The Parables: Their Literary and Existential Dimension* (Philadelphia:

When Christ spoke of "unrighteous mammon" he was underscoring the inherent fallenness of money. Unrighteousness is a necessary attribute of mammon. The word Jesus uses here (*adikos*) is very strong. Some translations render it "the mammon of iniquity," which perhaps best captures the odious character of the word. Commenting on this passage, Jacques Ellul has written, "This means both that Mammon generates and provokes iniquity and that Mammon, symbol of unrighteousness, emanates from iniquity. In any case, unrighteousness, the antithesis of God's word, is Mammon's trademark."[1]

The inherent unrighteousness of mammon is a hard pill for us to swallow. We so badly want to believe that mammon has no power over us, no authority of its own. But by giving the descriptive adjective *unrighteous* to mammon, Jesus forbids us from ever taking so naive a view of wealth. We must be more tough-minded, more realistic.

And in fact, those who work with money all the time know better than to think of it in neutral terms. As Jesus told us, in such matters the children of this world are wiser than the children of light (Luke 16:8). They know that money is far from harmless: money is poison, and if it is used in the wrong way, it can destroy as few things can. But they also know that once you conquer money

---

Fortress, 1967), and Donald Kraybill, in *The Upside Down Kingdom* (Scottdale, Penn.: Herald Press, 1978). To do this, however, not only takes the sting out of the parable, it makes it meaningless. The whole point of the teaching is that we are to take what is essentially "of this world" and use it in the service of God. This interpretation of "unrighteous mammon" is in complete accord with Jesus' other numerous negative statements regarding mammon.

Perhaps it should also be noted that some have sought to divorce the comments of Luke 16:8b–13 from the parable itself, viewing them as random pericopes that were gathered together and placed here. The statements, however, make sense *only* in relation to the parable as Jesus' commentary upon it.

and learn how to use it, its power is virtually unlimited. Money has power out of all proportion to its purchasing power. Because the children of this world understand this, they can use money for noneconomic purposes. And use it they do! Money is used as a weapon to bully people and to keep them in line. Money is used to "buy" prestige and honor. Money is used to enlist the allegiance of others. Money is used to corrupt people. Money is used for many things; it is one of the greatest powers in human society.

And this is precisely why Jesus tells us to "make friends" by means of this "unrighteous mammon." Rather than run from money, we are to take it—evil bent and all—and use it for kingdom purposes. We are to be absolutely clear about the venomous nature of money. But rather than reject it we are to conquer it and use it for noneconomic purposes. Money is to be captured, subdued, and used for greater goals. We are called to use money to advance the kingdom of God. What a tragedy it is if all we do is use money in the ordinary ways and not make any greater use of it.

MATTHEW 6

It is exactly this "greater use" that Jesus gives attention to in the sixth chapter of Matthew. He begins by warning us against "laying up treasures on earth"— mainly because it is such an insecure investment, for moth and rust will consume it, or thieves will steal it (Matt. 6:19). Rather, we are to lay up for ourselves "treasures in heaven," and we are to do so for two reasons. First, it is an investment that guarantees far greater security—neither moth, rust, thieves, nor any other thing can get to it. Second, it draws our affections—indeed our whole being—into the kingdom of God: "Where your treasure is, there will your heart be also" (Matt. 6:20-21).

Treasure in the bank of heaven is an investment with a high return.

It is often said of money that "you can't take it with you!" Jesus, however, is saying that if we know what we are doing we can take it with us after all. But how do we deposit treasure in heaven? We cannot deposit a check there.

One question to ask is, What will be in heaven? Obviously, there will be people in heaven; thus one way we lay up treasure in heaven is to invest in the lives of people. That kind of investment we will indeed take with us. Money invested in people is the best possible investment.

Suppose that the United States decided to change over its entire currency to British pounds, that the moment it did all American currency would be worthless, but that we were not told when the monetary conversion would take place. In that situation, the wise course would be to turn our money into British pounds, keeping only enough American currency to live day to day.

Now this gives us something of the picture Jesus means to convey when he tells us to lay up treasure in heaven and to make friends with unrighteous mammon. The proper use of money is not for living high down here; that would be a very poor investment indeed. No, the proper use of money is for investing as much of it as possible in the lives of people, so that we will have treasure in heaven. Of course, we need to keep a certain amount of money in order to carry on the day-to-day business of life, but we want to free up as much as we possibly can in order to place it where the return is eternal.

The children of light are faced with the great challenge of finding ways to convert "filthy lucre" into kingdom enterprises. Money, evil tendency and all, is to be mastered and turned into kingdom opportunities. Perhaps there is a needy neighbor next door, or a famine in the Sudan, or an opportunity to spread the gospel to a hitherto unreached group of people, or a chance to invest in the future of a bright young student. These are all wonderful investment opportunities.

USING, NOT SERVING

We can now bring into harmony the commandment of Matthew 6 that we are not to serve mammon and the counsel of Luke 16 that we are to make friends by means of unrighteous mammon. The Christian is given the high calling of *using* mammon without *serving* mammon. We are using mammon when we allow God to determine our economic decisions. We are serving mammon when we allow mammon to determine our economic decisions. We simply must decide who is going to make our decisions— God or mammon.

Do we buy a particular home on the basis of the call of God, or because of the availability of money? Do we buy a new car because we can afford it, or because God instructed us to buy a new car? If money determines what we do or do not do, then money is our boss. If God determines what we do or do not do, then God is our boss. My money might say to me, "You have enough to buy that," but my God might say to me, "I don't want you to have it." Now, who am I to obey?

Most of us allow money to dictate our decisions: what kind of house we live in, what vacation we will take, what job we will hold. Money decides.

Suppose Carolynn says to me, "Let's do this or that," and I complain, "But we don't have enough money!" What has happened? Money decided. You see, I did not say, "Well, honey, let's pray together and see if God wants us to do it." No, money made the decision. Money is my master. I am serving money.

J. Hudson Taylor would never have launched the great chapter in mission history called the China Inland Mission if he had let money decide. He was an ordinary person with few resources, yet once he had determined that God wanted him to go, he went. God had made the decision, not money. His master was God, and it was this master that he served.

Over the course of his effective ministry, God channeled very large sums of money through Hudson Taylor, enough to care for the needs of well over a thousand missionaries. But from his earliest days in the slums of London, Taylor had learned to understand money in the light of the cross. He had learned to use money without serving it.

And so the conflict we feel between Luke 16:9 and Matthew 6:24 is answered by learning to use money without serving money. But we must not be fooled: in the rough and tumble of life we find that the conflict is not resolved quickly or easily. Very often those who try to make friends by using mammon are soon serving mammon. We cannot safely use mammon until we are absolutely clear that we are dealing, not just with mammon, but with *unrighteous* mammon. The spiritual powers that stand in back of money and through which money lives and moves and has its being need to be conquered and subdued and made subservient to Jesus Christ. The conquest must go forth on all fronts at once, both inwardly and outwardly. We are seeking the overthrow of not only the spiritual power of mammon but the mammon spirit within us as well. The more we conquer money's evil side, the more money is used rather than served—and the more it is a blessing, not a curse.

MASTERING MAMMON

Just to say that we must master mammon does not make it happen. There are definite things we must do if we expect to defeat the tough old miser within and the spiritual powers without. The following steps in mastering mammon are given in the hope of starting you on your way.

The first step is to listen to the biblical witness about money. Begin with the Gospels. You may want to use a marking pen to highlight any reference to money and possessions. The purpose is to bathe in the biblical truth of Jesus' second most recurring theme. Next, turn to the Epistles with the same goal in mind. Then go back through all you have read and type up separately every reference to the dark side of money and every reference to the light side of money. Now that you can read the New Testament witness in one sitting, see what conclusions you can come to about money and write them down. Add any Old Testament passages about money that can give you added insight.

The second step is to consider money from a psychological and sociological perspective. We seek to understand ourselves better. Do we fear money? Do we hate money? Do we love money? Does money produce pride or shame in us?

We seek to understand our world better. What are the causes of Third World poverty and First World affluence? What responsibility do we bear for hurting, bleeding humanity? What resources are available to us?

As we grow in our understanding of the biblical, psychological, and sociological perspectives, we are able to turn to the third action step, which is the technical side, money management. Courageously we can take up such important items as family budgeting, estate planning, investments, deferred giving, and more. Now we can plan our budgets responsive to God's concern for the poor. Now we can evaluate our expenditures sensitive to a just sharing of the world's resources. Now we can write our wills unafraid of our own frailty. Now we can look at our giving in light of Christ's great missionary mandate. Now we can control and manage money to the glory of God and the good of others.

A fourth action step is to gather a community of support that will stand with us in our struggle and affirm us in life-style changes. Those who are rich and powerful need understanding and compassion as much as those who are poor and hungry.

A loving community of support can be found in many ways, and it does not always need to be formal or to take immense amounts of time. One January day I was having a brown-bag lunch with a judge and a businessman in our city, when the businessman pulled out a sheet of paper and began sharing with the two of us his giving goals for the next ten years. What fun to listen to his plans and sense his excitement in making his money count for the kingdom of God!

Husbands and wives can help each other. Home study groups can support one another. It is important, however, that such groups be quick to listen and slow to advise. Often an understanding heart is the greatest help we can give.

Such a community of creative, challenging, and affirming love may be slow in developing. Our wealth makes us lonely and isolated. What is needed is patience with each other and patience with ourselves. Our desire is to experience together the grace of a growing discipleship.

A fifth action step is to bring the ministry of prayer to bear directly upon money matters. Money *is* a spiritual issue, and prayer is our chief weapon in the life of the spirit. Let us learn to pray for each other for the binding of greed and covetousness and the releasing of liberality and generosity. In prayer, through the imagination, let us see the power of money broken. Let us picture the spiritual powers behind money brought under the lordship of Christ. Let us visualize money being channeled into needy lives, providing necessary food and medical supplies. Let us imagine Christians in business controlling, investing, and channeling money in new, creative, life-enhancing ways. Let us see the governments of the world diverting their vast resources away from bombs and into bread.

Let us pray for each other. We need wisdom to be faithful with our resources. It is a great service to lay hands on one another and pray for an increase of the gifts of wisdom and giving. Pray over how to budget money. Pray for freedom from money's power. Pray for money to be provided to those who need it. Before giving money away pray over it, asking God to use it for his good purposes: do the same for money that is invested in some enterprise.

Learn to pray preventive prayers. Rather than waiting until there is a financial problem, pray for protection of those who are doing well. If they have no money problems, pray that they will continue to know freedom. If they show the grace of giving, pray that the grace will increase. If they are called to manage and use money, surround them with the strong light of Christ so that they will be free from greed and avarice.

A sixth action step is to dethrone money.* By inner attitude and outward action, we must defile money's sacred character. Money is too high on our list of values. As Thomas Merton observed, "The true 'law' of our day is the law of wealth and material power."[2] For Christians, this giving of high priority to money is not just unfortunate, it is idolatry. For the sake of faithfulness to Christ, we need to find ways to shout no to the god money. We must dethrone it. One of the best ways is by showing

---

* See Jacques Ellul, *Money & Power* (Downers Grove. Ill.: Inter-Varsity Press, 1984) pp 109–16, for more on this subject

our disrespect for it. When we trample it under our feet we remove its power.

When Paul ministered the word of God in Ephesus, many people who had practicied "magic arts" brought their books and other objects and made a huge bonfire. Luke calculated that the estimated value of that act came to "fifty thousand pieces of silver" (Acts 19:18–20).

What they had done was profane something that in their world had become sacred. Without question, money has taken on a sacred character in our world, and it would do us good to find ways to defame it, defile it, and trample it under our feet.

So step on it. Yell at it. Laugh at it. List it way down on the scale of values—certainly far below friendship and cheerful surroundings. And engage in the most profane act of all—give it away. The powers that energize money cannot abide that most unnatural of acts, giving. Money is made for taking, for bargaining, for manipulating, but not for giving. This is exactly why giving has such ability to defeat the powers of money.

Not long ago we had a swing set, not one of those store-bought aluminum things but a real custom-made job—huge steel pipes and all. But our children would soon be beyond swing sets, so we decided that it would be good to sell it at a garage sale. My next decision was what price to put on it. I went out in the backyard and looked it over. "It should bring a good price," I thought to myself. "In fact, if I touched up the paint just a bit I could up the ante some, and if I fixed the seat on the glider I could charge even more . . ."

All of a sudden I began to monitor a spirit of covetousness within me, and I became aware of how really dangerous it was spiritually. Well, I went into the house and rather tentatively asked my wife, Carolynn, if she would mind if we gave the swing set away rather than selling it.

"No, not at all!" she responded quickly. I thought to my-self, "Rats!" But before the day was out we had found a couple with young children who could make good use of it, and we gave it to them—and I didn't even have to paint it! The simple act of giving crucified the greed that had gripped my heart, and the power of money was bro-ken—for the time being.

A seventh action step is to side with people against money and things. The biblical witness to this perspective is impressive. The Bible forbade charging interest on loans, because it was viewed as an exploitation of an-other's misfortune (e.g., Exod. 22:25). Wages were to be paid daily, because many people lived hand-to-mouth and needed the money (Deut. 24:14-15). When a coat was given as a pledge for borrowed tools, it was to be re-turned at night even if the tools had not been given back, because the nights were cold and the coat was needed (Deut. 24:6-13).

There are many things we can do to declare that we value people above things. We can be willing to lose money rather than a friendship. We can side with the "use" of church facilities over the "preservation" of facili-ties. We can provide wages that respond to human need as well as human productivity. We can always remember that the child who breaks the toy is more important than the toy. We can give up a major purchase to feed hungry people. The possibilities are endless.

One final action step: root out all favored treatment of people based upon money. James counsels us to "show no partiality" (James 2:1). He adds, "If a man with gold rings and in fine clothing comes into your assembly, and a poor man in shabby clothing also comes in, and you pay attention to the one who wears the fine clothing . . . have you not made distinctions among yourselves, and become judges with evil thoughts?" (James 2:2-4). Per-haps it is acceptable for political parties to give special privileges to generous benefactors, but such a practice can never be allowed in the community of faith. For believers, money can never be a bargaining tool or a way to gain status.

In the world money means access to the corridors of power; in the Church money should mean nothing. Money should not make people think better of us, for we are part of the fellowship of sinners. Money should not win us leadership roles, for those are determined by spiritual giftedness alone. Money should not make us more necessary to the fellowship, for our dependency is upon God, not money. In the fellowship of the Church money should mean nothing.

MONEY AND BUSINESS

In the first chapter I noted that business is the social side of money. In light of our analysis of money, what conclusions can we draw with regard to business?

As believers we affirm the goodness and necessity of work. Before the fall, Adam and Eve had generous work to do in the care of the garden. The curse that came from the fall was not work but work that was by the "sweat of your brow" (Gen. 3:19, kjv). That is, before the fall the fruits were commensurate to the effort, whereas after the fall the effort far exceeded the fruit gained.

When the apostle Paul said, "If any one will not work, let him not eat." (2 Thess. 3:10), he was not so much speaking against some welfare system as he was speaking for the goodness of work. We need to work. Work is creative, life-giving.

When Saint Benedict coined the phrase *Ora et labora*, Pray and work, he was calling attention to the intimate connection between the life of devotion and the life of labor. Work is essential to a spiritual life, and a spiritual life gives meaning to work.

As believers we affirm work that enhances human life and shun work that destroys human life. This brings us face-to-face with issues of immense importance and controversy. Is our ever increasing technology life-enhancing or dehumanizing? Can a Christian have any part in a military-industrial complex that produces weapons with obvious first-strike capability? Should we engage in occupations whose very nature involves compromises of many kinds? Is it ethical to work for companies that directly or indirectly destroy the ecological balance on the earth?

You can see that the vocational question is much broader than whether or not a Christian should be a bartender. In the first church I pastored, a faithful member—a brilliant Ph.D. in physics—came to me deeply disturbed because he had just learned that 80 percent of the research at the think tank where he worked ended up being used for military purposes. The job was death-giving! Yet it was the very work for which he had given half his life to become qualified to perform. Difficult decisions indeed!

Many jobs are clearly more life-enhancing than others. Teaching, counseling, pastoring—these obviously place us smack in the middle of human need and afford precious opportunities to bring a redemptive touch. But there are many more possibilities. All the people-related tasks—from child care worker to medical doctor—provide excellent opportunities to enhance human life. Often these helping professions pay less, have less prestige, and are more demanding, but they should be highly valued in the Christian fellowship because of their life-changing potential. A preschool teacher is doing much more than making a living; he or she is molding lives. Purpose and meaning in one's work can be fringe benefits of the highest order.

All the occupations that provide needed services and manufacture needed goods are life-enhancing. Farmers, carpenters, electricians, grocery store clerks, and many others enrich us in innumerable ways. We need them all.

The arts is another life-enhancing field. Music and drama, film and sculpture, literature and art enrich the human experience and need to be captured for the cause of Christ. The day is long overdue for the Christian fellowship to once again gain an exalted view of the arts.

We could profit from a fresh look at the Puritan emphasis upon "calling" in our vocation. Prayer groups and "clearness meetings" could be gathered to help *all* the members of the fellowship—not just potential pastors—find their vocational place.

There are many other jobs I could have mentioned and many questions related to the jobs I did mention. Computer technology, law, science, and many other fields need to be studied in the light of this affirmation.

As believers we affirm human value above economic value. For the Christian, the bottom line can never be the bottom line. An employee is more than just the cost of production. There are human needs that take precedence over monetary needs.

Business people face many tough questions. Return on investment must be given careful attention, for no business can survive long if it sees only red on the ledger sheet. To go bankrupt helps no one. But profits must be brought into perspective alongside many other equally important values.

The principle of human value above economic value will have a lot to say about how we organize a business. For example, some businesses organize in such a way that periodic layoffs are virtually guaranteed. Recognizing this as a human problem, we might place a higher priority on trying to balance contracts so as to achieve greater stability.

Many American corporations are set up on the assumption of high employee turnover. Some companies even build-in a high turnover rate on purpose so that wages can be kept lower. Japanese corporations, on the other hand, tend to organize for low employee turnover. It is not easy to deal with the problem of mobility in a culture, but if we begin with a different set of assumptions, we might well make a big difference.

If we assume longer employee tenure, that will affect how we handle wages, employee benefits, and retirement programs. Even more, it will mean that we will place a high priority on people developing friendships and establishing networks of support.

The Japanese model has shown us that long-term stability does not need to conflict with profits; in fact, in many ways it seems to enhance them. But even if that were not the case, Christians have an obligation to place concern for human beings into their ledger calculations.

As believers we affirm the need to enter into each other's space in the employer–employee relationship. Let us not fool ourselves: employers and employees are involved in a power relationship. Employers have the power to fire and hire, to raise or lower wages, to control benefits and working conditions. The employee has the power to frustrate or enhance the working relationship and, in some cases, to undermine the effective functioning of the company.

Employers need to *feel* the insecurity of employees. Very often employees feel dehumanized and used, and very often they are. Mechanization that is done to ensure efficiency can depersonalize the entire enterprise.

In an act of Christian identification, employers can stand in the place of their employees. They can try to feel what it is like to have someone else controlling their future. Do you buy the new refrigerator if a layoff is impending? Do you add on the extra bedroom if there is the possibility of a transfer? Asking themselves questions like these can help employers feel what it is like to be an employee.

This does not mean that painful decisions cannot be

made. Employers must still look at income and expenses and overall production. Decisions may look terribly cold at the time, yet if they are made in the context of an ongoing identification with the employee's vulnerability, a measure of grace can permeate the situation, and wrong and harmful decisions often can be avoided.

Employees, in turn, need to *feel* the isolation of employers. Leadership and responsibility set a person apart in many ways. Everyone knows that criticism is the price of leadership, but that does not make it hurt less. The old adage that sticks and stones may break our bones but names will never hurt us is simply not true.

As employees seek to stand in the shoes of employers, questions begin to surface. If I had to be concerned for the good of the entire enterprise, would my evaluation of what needs to be done change? How would it feel to live with a business around the clock rather than merely eight to five? In what ways do status and wealth decrease life's pleasures?

Trying to understand the dilemmas of employers does not mean that criticism should be avoided. For the good of employers, criticism is necessary. A perceptive challenge to a long-standing practice can lead to creative new ideas. But once we have entered into the lonely space of our superiors, our criticism will be tempered with understanding.

As believers we refuse to buy or sell things frivolous. Fads will come and go; there is no need for the follower of Christ to participate.

John Woolman, who owned and operated a retail goods store, wrote of his own struggles with this. In 1756 he noted in his Journal, "It had been my general practice to buy and sell things really useful. Things that served chiefly to please the vain mind in people, I was not easy to trade in; seldom did it; and whenever I did I found it weakened me as a Christian."[3]

Our refusal to merchandise in the frivolous is directly connected to the high value we place upon human life. It is a wrong use of the world's resources to fritter them away on trivialities when human beings need to be fed, clothed, and educated. We value people more than ostentatious clothes and gaudy homes. So long as the gospel needs to be preached, so long as children need to be fed, Christians cannot afford to have any part with the "Vanity Fairs" of this world.

However, no clear lines can be drawn between things frivolous and things essential. What is an unnecessary luxury to one person is a necessity to another. What is superfluous at one time becomes indispensable in another context.

Though the difficulties are genuine, they should not obscure the fact that many issues are really quite clear. In many cases we need, not more insight, but strength to obey what we already know is right. We can quickly turn away from many things as evidences of the old life. In the few cases in which we have honest questions, we may ask guidance of the Lord, who gives his wisdom liberally, and we may also ask discerning members of the Christian fellowship, who can often bring us the word of the Lord. Of course, we will have to struggle with many money matters, holding in creative tension the many needs, opportunities, and responsibilities that make up our world. Only fools imagine that it could or should be otherwise.

As believers we refuse to take advantage of our neighbor. How to hammer this out on the hard anvil of the business world is no small task, but hammer it out we must. Yet many of the situations we face are completely unambiguous. Recently my wife and I sold a car that had chronic carburetor problems. Both of us were clear that whoever looked at it had to be told of the problem and encouraged to have a mechanic give an evaluation. We probably sold it for considerably less than perhaps we could have, but integrity and friendship are worth a great deal. The point is to stick to plain statements without attempts to embellish or obscure the truth.

In many business situations contracts are good and help us to keep from taking advantage of our neighbor. A contract accomplishes several things. It puts the agreement into writing, so that miscommunication is minimized. The lawyers who help draft the contract often can see potential problems that we who are not schooled in "legalese" have missed. Also, a contract forces us to clarify in our own minds what we are doing.

Contracts, therefore, are good, but trust is better. Contracts are a witness to the fall and the natural tendency to sin. Trust is a witness to grace and the supernatural tendency toward righteousness. One of the greatest evils of a contract is its tendency to breed distrust and suspicion that often ends up in lawsuits. Paul counseled against going to court to settle disputes and we would be wise to avoid it whenever possible (1 Cor. 6:1-11).

Trust, by contrast, builds community. To be sure, when we trust, we run the risk of having others take advantage of us. However, note that I did not state the principle to our defense but to the defense of others. We refuse never to take advantage of our neighbor; that is no guarantee that our neighbors will not take advantage of us. In fact, they *will* take advantage of us. But trust is worth the risk because of its power to build community. Besides, as Paul put it, "Why not . . . suffer wrong? Why not . . . be defrauded?" (1 Cor. 6:7). And why not? After all, it is only money, and there are many things of far greater value than money.

As Christians our word is as good as our bond. Others may well take advantage of us, but perhaps, just perhaps, our willingness to be defrauded rather than to break the bonds of community can witness to a better way.

These six principles, then, can frame the beginning of

a growing understanding of the role of the Christian in business:

- —As believers we affirm the goodness and the necessity of work.
- —As believers we affirm work that enhances human life and shun work that destroys human life.
- —As believers we affirm human value above economic value.
- —As believers we affirm the need to enter into each other's space in the employer-employee relationship.
- —As believers we refuse to buy or sell things frivolous.
- —As believers we refuse to take advantage of our neighbor.

UNITY AT THE MANGER

We have seen that the Bible emphasizes both a dark and a light side with regard to money. The gulf between the two can seem very large indeed, but we have worked to bridge the gap.

Now come with me to the manger in Bethlehem. Notice the worshipers—humble shepherds and regal magi. Here we see poverty and wealth both brought to the manger. The kingly gifts of gold, frankincense, and myrrh are given freely in the service of the messianic King. Shepherds who have been closed out of life's money channels give their presence and their worship. Both are called, the poorest of the poor and the richest of the rich. Both come, both kneel, both give Christmas worship.

5. The Vow of Simplicity

> Simplicity is an uprightness of soul.
> —FRANÇOIS FÉNELON

In the past three chapters we have been dealing with the difficult—our wealth. We have been learning to overcome our resistance, to claim our richness, and to share it with new freedom and joy.

Our study of money leads us to one inescapable conclusion: we who follow Jesus Christ are called to a vow of simplicity. This vow is not for the dedicated few but for all. It is not an option to take or leave depending on our personal preference. All who name Christ as Lord and Savior are obliged to follow what he says, and Jesus' call to discipleship in money can be best summed up in the single word *simplicity*. Simplicity seeks to do justice to our Lord's many-faceted teachings about money—light and dark, giving and receiving, trust, contentment, faith.

Simplicity means unity of heart and singleness of purpose. We have only one desire: to obey Christ in all things. We have only one purpose: to glorify Christ in all things. We have only one use for money: to advance his kingdom upon the earth. Jesus declares, "If thine eye be single thy whole body shall be full of light" (Matt. 6:22, KJV).

Simplicity means joy in God's good creation. Oscar Wilde once said that people do not value sunsets because they cannot pay for them. Not so for us! We cherish all the free gifts of the good earth: sunset and sunrise, land and sea, colors and beauty everywhere.

Simplicity means contentment and trust. "Have no anxiety about anything" counsels Paul (Phil. 4:6). "Having nothing, and yet possessing everything" (2 Cor. 6:10). "I have learned, in whatever state I am, to be content" (Phil. 4:11). This is the way Paul lived, and so do we.

Simplicity means freedom from covetousness. Paul's confession is ours, "I coveted no one's silver or gold" (Acts 20:33). We no longer "pant after the possessions of others," as John Calvin put it![1]

Simplicity means modesty and temperance in all things. Paul calls us to be "sober, just, holy, temperate" (Titus 1:8, KJV). And so we are. Our lives are marked by voluntary abstinence in the midst of extravagant luxury. We refuse to indulge in elegance and display in clothing or manner of life. Our use of resources is always tempered by human need.

Simplicity means to receive material provision gratefully. Through Isaiah, God promises, "If you are willing and obedient, you shall eat the good of the land" (Isa. 1:19). We are not rigid ascetics who cannot abide a land flowing with milk and honey. Rather, we rejoice in these gracious provisions from the heart of God. Complete personal deprivation is not a good thing, and we reject it as a sign of duplicity, not simplicity.

Simplicity means using money without abusing money. In the power of the Holy Spirit we conquer and capture money and put it into service for Christ and his kingdom. We know that well-being is not defined by wealth, and so we can hold all things lightly—owning without treasuring, possessing without being possessed. We use money within the confines of a properly disciplined spiritual life, and we manage money for the glory of God and the good of all people.

Simplicity means availability. Freed from the compulsions of ever bigger and ever better, we have the time and energy to respond to human need. Some, like pastors and others, are freed full-time so they can minister the word of life. Others will release blocks of time to further advance the kingdom.

Simplicity means giving joyfully and generously. We give ourselves, and we give the product of our life's work. "First they gave themselves," said Paul of the churches of Macedonia (2 Cor. 8:5). The matter of giving is so central to our entire relationship toward money that I would like us to turn our attention to a more detailed discussion of this aspect of simplicity.

GUIDELINES FOR GIVING

When we read the teaching of the Bible concerning money we see very quickly that giving figures very prominently. We would be hard pressed to find a teaching on money that does not somehow mention giving. Whether we think of the tithe, the law of gleaning, the Jubilee principle, the story of Zacchaeus, the story of the rich young ruler, the parable of the good Samaritan, the parable of the rich fool, or any number of other passages, we find a strong emphasis upon giving.

If we take the biblical witness seriously, it seems that one of the best things we can do with money is to give it away. The reason is obvious: giving is one of our chief weapons in conquering the god mammon. Giving scandalizes the world of commerce and competition. It wins money for the cause of Christ. Jacques Ellul has noted, "We have very clear indications that money, in the Christian life, is made *in order* to be given away."[2] Hence the guidelines that follow are an attempt to help us in our giving.

First, with glad and generous hearts let us give proportionately, beginning with a tithe of our incomes. Neither Jesus nor any of the apostles confined giving to the tithe—they went beyond it. In all their teachings, generosity and sacrifice loom large. This is true whether we are looking at the poor widow giving her mite or Barnabas giving a parcel of land to the early church (Mark 12:41-44; Acts 4:36-37).

The tithe, therefore, is an Old Testament principle that should be a standard we will not go below except in the rarest of circumstances. This is not a rigid law, but a starting point for organizing our economic lives.

Now it takes no financial wizard to determine 10 percent of our gross income, but it demands a deep sensitivity to the Spirit of God to know what proportionate giving means. In wrestling with this matter, Elizabeth O'Connor has written: "Proportionate to what? Proportionate to the accumulated wealth of one's family? Proportionate to one's income and the demands upon it, which vary from family to family? Proportionate to one's sense of security and the degree of anxiety with which one lives? Proportionate to the keenness of our awareness of those who suffer? Proportionate to our sense of justice and of God's ownership of all wealth? Proportionate to our sense of stewardship for those who follow after us? And so on, and so forth. The answer, of course, is in proportion to all of these things."[3]

To help us think through what proportionate giving might mean, Ron Sider has suggested the concept of the graduated tithe.[4] Very simply, one decides on a standard of living and tithes 10 percent on that amount. Then, out of every thousand dollars of additional income, one gives 5 percent more. With this arrangement, once we have reached eighteen thousand dollars of income above our standard, we give away 100 percent of all additional income.

One man I know has another approach. He owns a business and has put himself on a salary that he has determined as his standard of living. Of this salary he tithes 15 percent. He then gives away 25 percent of the profits that the company generates above his salary. He also has income from book and film royalties and speaking honorariums; he gives away a hundred percent of this money.

Perhaps some of us with ample resources should try living on 10 percent of our income and giving away 90 percent. R. G. LeTourneau, owner of a large earth-moving business, did this very thing.

But please, do not be intimidated by these examples. They are only illustrations of ways we can come to terms with proportionate giving in an affluent culture. Many of us need to take smaller, more humble steps. Some have disciplined themselves to match dollar for dollar what they spend on lawn fertilizer with fertilizer for Third World food production. Others might want to match money spent on eating out with giving to famine-relief projects or match money spent on clothes with giving to a relief agency. The idea is simply to inform our spending with a sensitivity to the needs of others.

Perhaps none of these ideas are right for you. Many people feel so strapped financially that the idea of giving "above and beyond" seems ludicrous. And yet many of us can do much more if we begin to think in creative new ways.

One word of caution: some people need to give *less* than they do now if they are to be faithful to God. You may need to care for your children or your parents or your spouse—or even yourself—more adequately. Do not excuse your responsibility on religious pretenses. Jesus, you remember, had very strong words for such a practice (Mark 7:9-13).

Second, with glad and generous hearts, let us keep in creative tension "reasoned" giving and "risk" giving. There is one kind of giving that carefully evaluates the track record of organizations and individuals, and another that gives without calculation. Both kinds of giving are essential.

A good percentage of our giving should be reasoned and responsible. If we are giving to organizations, many questions need to be asked. Does the organization to which I am giving have a good record of responsible use of money? How much goes to overhead, and how much gets to the project to which I am giving? Does the organization have a responsible board that monitors the use of money? Is there an annual audit? Is the organization a member of the Evangelical Council for Financial Accountability?

If our giving is to individuals, another set of questions needs to be considered. Will my giving be helpful, or harmful? What is the right amount for that person to receive? Does he or she have an overall budget? Is this to be a one-time gift, or a regular monthly gift? What other sources of income does this person have or should have? Can I give to someone without controlling that person?

However, there is a danger in too much calculation in our giving. That danger is the subtle tendency to call the shots. The warm openness that once characterized our giving can gradually turn into tightfistedness. A miserly spirit becomes justified in the name of prudent and responsible giving.

To overcome this soul-destroying bid for power we need to give with lavish abandon, like the woman with the alabaster jar (Matt. 26:6-13). In an act of uncalculated generosity she broke it and poured its treasure on Christ's head. The disciples saw it as an act of waste; Jesus saw it as an act of beauty.

For the sake of our own souls there are times when we need to throw caution to the winds and give, just give. We need to risk giving to individuals, not because they have proven that they can handle money well, but because they need it. In so doing, we give love and trust as well. And we free ourselves from that clutching, holding spirit that spells spiritual ruin.

Third, with glad and generous hearts let us seek out and give to individuals and organizations that lack celebrity status. We are so often prone to champion causes that already have thousands of champions. But among the disciples of Christ this is not to be. We are to seek out and generously support the disenfranchised and the disinherited.

Let us discover the politically uninteresting, the "newsworthyless," and lend our hand of support. These are not found on television or in newspapers or in magazines. These are found by prayerfully walking into the press of humanity. Ask God to give you eyes to see and ears to hear the little ones of the kingdom—the ones others normally pass by without a second thought.

We need a divine sense of foresight rather than hindsight when it comes to supporting God's servants. George Mueller began giving to support J. Hudson Taylor long before Taylor won fame as a pioneer missionary. There were no enthusiastic cover stories in the Christian magazines about Taylor's outlandish proposal to go into the interior of China with an army of missionaries. But Mueller found in this young man a soul hard after God. We now look back at Hudson Taylor as inaugurating the second great wave in the modern missionary movement.

To have the foresight that Mueller had demands a spiritual perception born out of intimate communion with the Heavenly Monitor and the courage to go into the highways and byways of life to discover the work of God.

How do we get beyond the media propaganda machine into places of kingdom need and action? Begin by inviting every missionary you can into your home to share their insights and broaden your cross-cultural vision. These faithful workers are a tremendous resource of wisdom and experience, but often they are neglected because we confine them to the one forum they are least prepared for—public speaking. But bring them into your home and ask them where God's work is going forward, and these quiet, mild-mannered folk turn instantly into fiery orators.

As you go about your daily routine, listen prayerfully to people—ideas and needs crop up in the strangest places. Gather in small study groups and ask, What is God doing in our world? As you gather with others for worship, invite those with prophetic insight to help you see the direction you are headed, show you where that leads, and give you a value judgment upon it. Take your summer vacation among the huddled masses of Haiti instead of on a cruise to Puerto Vallarta. In these and many other ways, we can try to find the unsung heroes and the unrecorded places where the battle is hottest.

Fourth, with glad and generous hearts, let us give without seeking power. We do not need to control, to manage, or to influence. Freely we have received, freely we give.

In Acts we see the generous giving of the early church that broke the cycle of tyranny by which benefactors dictated terms to the poor and powerless. Money was used by the early church, not as an instrument of control, but as an instrument of love. All the subtle tricks were gone. And when someone did attempt a financial power play, it was quickly revealed for the sin it was and speedily dealt with (Acts 5:1-11). It should be so among us.

As disciples we reject money's manipulative capacity. We refuse to use money to jockey for position or to maneuver ourselves into favor. We will not pull strings or put anyone into our debt with money. We reject money's power for evil; we affirm money's power for good.

Our pastors and others need to know of our faithful support, even if they do and say things we do not like. They can thus be encouraged to fulfill their prophetic ministry. Otherwise, they will hesitate to speak unpopular words and to espouse unwelcome programs for fear of crippling the work economically. They need to know that our giving is not determined by the latest public opinion poll. We will not hold the Church ransom because we disagree with this or that decision.

There may, of course, come a time when it is appropriate to withhold our giving out of concern for the direction of our local congregation, but that comes a long way down the road. The normal pattern is to give freely without any need to direct how the Church is using the money. I can well imagine that the poor widow could have thought of plenty of reasons to withhold her "mite" from the temple treasury. Yet she gave, and Jesus honored the act (Mark 12:41-44).

Fifth, with glad and generous hearts, let us give ourselves as well as our money. "First they gave themselves," declared Paul (2 Cor. 8:5). And so must we.

Someone I know who always has given of his resources generously is attempting now to give more of himself. He decided that he needed a closer personal tie to the poor, so instead of just writing checks to organizations that work among the poor, he decided to make a commitment to one family. This family has known little stability over the years, because of drugs and related problems. But with this man's help, the husband has secured a job and the family has learned to live by a monthly budget and a weekly food menu. My friend meets with the family every week to review their budget with them and evaluate their goals. He also has had to invest some of his own resources in the family (none of it is tax deductible). This kind of giving is much more costly than writing a check, yet giving oneself along with money can produce dramatic results.

Someone else I know has used his resources to establish a Christian film company, a publishing house, and a seminary. These projects take up a tremendous amount of his time and energy, but he does it because he wants to give himself as well as his money.

These two examples may seem more than most of us can do. But there are many simple and humble ways to give ourselves. In Acts we read of Tabitha, who made "coats and garments" for the widows of her village. Luke describes her as "full of good works and acts of charity" (Acts 9:36-43). Perhaps we also can discover ways to give ourselves by meeting the needs of those around us, so that we too will be full of good works and acts of charity.

Sixth, with glad and generous hearts, let us seek out advisers who can help us in our giving.[5] It is responsible stewardship to seek out the finest expertise available to guide us with regard to outright cash gifts, deferred giving, wills, planned giving, and more so that our total estate is seen in perspective. This can be done informally through Bible classes and casual visits or formally through hired financial planners.

One warning is in order. Most financial advisers are by temperament and spirit conservative and technical in orientation. Their technical knowledge of the money world is vitally important, but, for the believer, facts and figures can never speak the last word. A free and liberated spirit is essential throughout the process. Very few lawyers and trust officers—even those with a Christian orientation—understand the spiritual nature of money or the spirit of carefree unconcern that is to characterize our lives. And so, though we can be grateful for their counsel and advice, we cannot be bound by it.

Remember that laying up treasure in heaven is a major business investment. As in any serious venture, we want to do the very best we can. Most of us will have hundreds of thousands of dollars flowing through our hands in the course of our employable years. As stewards we have a responsibility to use this bounty in ways that will reap the greatest benefit for Christ and his kingdom. Each of us will have to work through our own priorities for kingdom investments, and advisers can help us find our way.

By these comments I do not in the least mean to depreciate the use of money in the service of one's family. Quite to the contrary, I think one of the finest investments I can make for advancing the kingdom of God upon the earth is that of investing in my own children. Enriching experiences that broaden their perspective and sensitize their spirit are well worth the investment.

Seventh, with glad and generous hearts, let us make out caring wills that express our concern for the kingdom of God. It is understandable that people hesitate to make out a will. It shouts out to us about our finitude and makes specific our resources—realities most of us would like to avoid. But the failure to draw up a will is the worst possible stewardship. Our denial of our wealth has been so constant and so total that most of us would be astonished at the resources we could potentially make available to the world upon our graduation into heaven. I say "potentially" because without a will those resources will be lost to the work of God.

So if you have no will, make an appointment to draw one up before you finish this chapter. Do not excuse yourself on the grounds that you are too young to die or do not have enough money to make any difference. Both statements are false, so draw up a will right away.

The Church could do an immense service by offering instruction sessions in how to handle this matter. It is the best possible context in which to face up to both our wealth and our impending death. Besides, many questions could be meaningfully addressed in a Christian context. Do I leave all my resources to my children, or only a percentage? What organizations could I include in my will that would best advance the cause of Christ? Are there ways I could give to the poor in death that I cannot do in life?

In our will, Carolynn and I have included our children, to be sure. But we have also included educational institutions, mission organizations, relief organizations, and churches. Many others have done much more. Some have even left an intangible witness. Patrick Henry wrote into his will that if he had left nothing in terms of worldly riches but had given his heirs a faith in Jesus Christ, then they were of all people most wealthy. Conversely, he added that if he had left them all the wealth in the world but had not left them a faith in Jesus Christ, they would be of all people most destitute.

Please believe me, wills are nothing to fear. You can help so many with so little effort that I cannot conceive of a valid reason to postpone writing one.

Giving is a glad and generous ministry to which we are all called. In times of persecution Christians give their lives; in times of prosperity Christians give the fruit of their life's work. William Law said of the early Christian fellowship that they "were glad to turn their whole estates into a constant course of charity."[6] How wonderful if that could be a description of us as well!

As we learn and grow in the ministry of giving, I do want to raise a word of warning. Money, like crabgrass, has a way of rerooting itself in our hearts. We think we have dethroned it and made it an obedient servant, and then all of a sudden it subversively attempts a coup. At its core money seems to have a rebellious nature.

Over the years my friend Don has had an effective ministry with money—earning and giving.* A few years ago he decided to make his giving a capital enterprise. He would buy a piece of property for, say, five thousand dollars and later resell it for perhaps ten thousand and thus be able to give twice as much as he would have otherwise. He was managing money for the greater gain of Christ and his kingdom.

In time, however, Don noticed that he was beginning

---

* The name has been changed to maintain confidentiality.

to be captivated by an investment mentality—a kind of greed for the kingdom. The sense of warmhearted giving began to dry up and become utilitarian giving. Beyond this, giving of long-term capital gains meant that he had to hold onto the property for at least one year, and as he told me, "In that year of waiting you begin to be attached to the money." Don is still working through the spiritual barrenness that has resulted from this process.

Don began this ministry with the most honorable of intentions. And fortunately, he has a sensitive enough spirit to know when the power of money is reasserting itself. We all need to be forewarned and equipped as we enter this dangerous ministry. Money—unrighteous mammon—is poison, and like poison, it is a blessing only when it is used properly and with great care.*

CHILDREN AND MONEY

As disciples of Christ, we cannot avoid the task of teaching our children and the children in our fellowship about money. We cannot hide them from money, for it permeates the very atmosphere of the world in which they live. Some parents may find it embarrassing to talk to their children about sex, but that is nothing compared to our reluctance to openly confront the issue of money.

The truth is, of course, that we *will* teach our children about money. Our very reluctance teaches. Who we are and the daily transactions of ordinary life form the content of our teaching. Our children will pick up from us an all-pervasive attitude toward money.

> Should I fear money?
> Should I love money?
> Should I respect money?

---

* Those who invest money will find a helpful guide to justice in investments in the July 1984 issue of *The Other Side* magazine.

Should I hate money?
Should I use money?
Should I borrow money?
Should I budget money?
Should I sacrifice everything for money?

All these questions and more are answered for children as they watch us. Albert Schweitzer once observed, "There are only three ways to teach a child: the first is by example, the second is by example, the third is by example."[7]

If we are free from the love of money, our children will know it. If apprehension is our automatic response to money, we will teach them worry and fear.

Children need instruction in both the dark and the light side of money. Without this, teaching them how to make a budget and write checks is of little value.

It is not difficult to instruct children about the light side of money. They quickly learn of its ability to bring them many good things. We help them see how money can also be a blessing to others. We give them jobs to do, provide an allowance, teach them to tithe and to save, show them how to use money wisely. Slowly we give them increased control and liberty as they learn how to deal responsibly with money. This—and much more— forms the curriculum for our instruction on the light side of money.

Instruction on the dark side of money is more difficult. For children, the power to buy is heady stuff. Children from poor backgrounds know the evil of too little and cannot imagine too much having an evil side. Children from affluent backgrounds find tremendous power in humiliating their less fortunate friends, never imagining they themselves are also just as unfortunate. The very idea that money is a spiritual power seeking to enslave seems ludicrous to them.

But we must teach them. And more than teach, we

must pray for their deliverance from money's domination. This is no light matter. Money is not just a thing—it is a power. The moment we expose our children to money—and expose them we must—we should pray for their protection.

We also teach. When children fight over money, we can use the opportunity to help them see money's power. We can show them real poverty and help them consider the causes of inequity in the world.

We teach them by word and deed that money is neither respectable nor contemptible. We owe money no honor, but neither do we despise it. Money is useful, even necessary, but it is not to be esteemed or admired. In short, we try to show children how to use money without serving money (e.g., Luke 16:9 and Matt. 6:24).

This distinction is difficult to teach children mainly because so few adults know the difference. We live in an age in which right discipline and control over one's life are so little understood that obsession and abstinence are the only categories that make sense for the modern mind. Either we reject a thing out of hand or we accept it without reservation. This is why dogmatism is so popular today—whether in religion, politics, or economics.

It is precisely this that makes it so incumbent upon us to teach children *use without abuse* in all of life. We show them by example that it is quite possible to watch a single television program and then turn the set off, to eat what is required for good health and then stop, to enjoy good music and then experience silence.

Once children see from us that it is possible to exercise restraint over human passions, then it will be possible to convey the notion of money as servant rather than master. That is the first step, but only the first. Much more must be taught.

For example, children need to know how to exercise authority over the spiritual power of money. We need to

help them flesh out answers to many questions. What
actions defeat selfishness? How do you effectively pray
against greed? How do you release the spirit of generosity
and compassion?

Most of all, we are to teach children how to profane
money without rejecting it. Let us learn to laugh at its
pious religiosity. Let us desecrate its sacred shrines.
How? One way is to despise and utterly reject the propaganda that "more is better." Here is where, as parents,
we must really fight the battle. A child tends to feel that,
if one toy is satisfying, two or three or four will be more
satisfying. But we know that this is not necessarily the
case. And in this regard we must learn to be as tough as
nails, knowing that no is a good answer. Enough is
enough, and we should say so to ourselves and to our
children. We buy something because we need it, not because we want it, and our children need to learn the difference.

Money does not deserve our respect. It deserves to be
conquered in the power of the Spirit. Once defeated and
converted to the way of Christ, it can then be used without being served.

GENEROSITY, MAGNANIMITY, AND SHALOM

The dark side of money inevitably leads to greed,
which leads to vengeance, which leads to violence. The
light side of money inevitably leads to generosity, which
leads to magnanimity, which leads to shalom.[8]

The great moral question of our time is how to move
from greed to generosity, and from vengeance to magnanimity, and from violence to shalom. The vow of simplicity points the way. Simplicity gives us the perspective
and the courage to stand against greed, vengeance, and

violence. Simplicity gives us the framework to experience generosity, magnanimity, and shalom. Saint Francis de Sales said, "I recommend to you holy simplicity. . . . In everything, love simplicity."[9]

PART II
Sex

6. Sexuality and Spirituality

> Sexuality and spirituality are not enemies but friends.
> —DONALD GOERGEN

One of the real tragedies in Christian history has been the divorce of sexuality from spirituality. This fact is all the more lamentable since the Bible holds such a high celebrative view of human sexuality. Let us look at some of the biblical windows onto human sexuality.

MALE AND FEMALE

In the first chapter of Genesis we have a brief, yet magnificent, comment on the meaning of human sexuality. The narrative opens in majesty as God brings the universe into existence by speaking the creative word. And this universe that he created is good, very good. (Please, let us get it straight once and for all: the material world is good and not to be despised. We urgently need to recover a doctrine of God as Creator and of a creation that is good, very good.)

Human beings are the apex of God's creation. In simple, yet noble, language we are told that the human creation is set apart from all others, for it is in the *imago Dei*, the image of God. Notice how closely related our human sexuality is to the *imago Dei*: "So God created man in his own image, in the image of God he created him; *male and female he created them*" (Gen. 1:27, emphasis mine). Strange as it may seem, our sexuality, our maleness and femaleness, is somehow related to our creation in the image of God.

Karl Barth was the first major theologian to help us see

the implications of this tremendous confession of Scripture that human sexuality is grounded in the *imago Dei*. What he has helped us understand is that relationship is at the heart of what it means to be "in the image of God" and that the relationship between male and female is the human expression of our relationship with God.

Our human sexuality, our maleness and femaleness, is not just an accidental arrangement of the human species, not just a convenient way to keep the human race going. No, it is at the center of our true humanity. We exist as male and female in relationship. Our sexualness, our capacity to love and be loved, is intimately related to our creation in the image of God. What a high view of human sexuality!

Notice too that the biblical stress upon relationship helps to enlarge our understanding of human sexuality. The problem with the topless bars and the pornographic literature of our day is not that they emphasize sexuality too much but that they do not emphasize it enough. They totally eliminate relationship and restrain sexuality to the narrow confines of the genital. They have made sex trivial.

How much richer and fuller is the biblical perspective! To chat over coffee, to discuss a great book, to view a sunset together—this is sexuality at its best, for male and female are in intimate relationship. To be sure, genital sex is a part of the total picture, but human sexuality is a far larger reality than merely coitus.

NAKED AND NOT ASHAMED

God spoke all of the creation into existence except for human beings.* To create Adam he took the dust of the

---

* Barth feels that the second creation narrative (Gen. 2:18-25) has as its basic purpose to fill out the theme of our creation as male and female, so that in a sense it is a commentary upon Gen. 1:27.

earth and breathed life into it (Gen. 2:7). And that union of earthy dust and divine breath gives us one of the finest descriptions of human nature. God did not speak Eve into existence as though she were a part of nonhuman reality, nor did he breathe into dust as though she were a creation unrelated to man. God used the rib of Adam to underscore their interdependence—"bone of my bones and flesh of my flesh," as Adam expressed it. The two of them interwoven, interdependent, interlaced: no fierce rivalry, no hierarchical one-upmanship, no independent autonomy. What a beautiful picture.

Next we are given the confession of covenant fidelity that sets the pattern for mature marriage: "Therefore a man leaves his father and his mother and cleaves to his wife, and they become one flesh" (Gen. 2:24). This is really an extraordinary statement. Given the intensely patriarchal culture, it is genuinely phenomenal for a biblical author to speak of the man "leaving" and "cleaving." Then the Bible describes their joining as a "one flesh" reality, a phrase to which Jesus gives depth and richness in his teaching.

Finally, the scene closes with the most refreshing comment of all: "And the man and his wife were both naked, and were not ashamed" (Gen. 2:25). Here we have an idyllic picture of two whose sexuality was integrated into their entire lives. There was no shame because there was wholeness. There was an organic unity within themselves and with the rest of creation. Lewis Smedes has written, "There are two situations in which people feel no shame. The first is in a state of wholeness. The other is in a state of illusion."[1] Naked and not ashamed—a magnificent scene.

Did you notice that unashamed eroticism existed before the fall? The fall did not create eros; it only perverted it. In the creation story we find the man and the woman drawn to each other, naked and not ashamed. They know their masculinity and femininity are the handiwork of God, as is their passionate affection. Their differences also unite them; they are male and female but also one flesh. The two of them in relationship, in love—why should there be shame? Their sexuality is the creation of God.

We all know the tragic conclusion to the story, how the man and the woman rejected God's way. And the venom of that fall poisoned everything. It ruptured the relationship between God and Adam and Eve. It even soured the marriage relationship. In the language of the curse, the man "shall rule over you" (Gen. 3:16). We must never forget that the domination of women by men that fills our history books and our current events is not a part of God's good creation but a result of the fall; hence the tension, the conflict, the hierarchy. As David Hubbard has noted, since the fall "human life has vacillated between the grasping femininity which competes with man and man's blind dominion over woman which degrades personality and destroys partnership."[2]

The result for human sexuality has been, as Karl Barth put it, a vacillation between evil eroticism, on the one hand, and an evil absence of eroticism, on the other. How tragic! However, the Christian witness is that with the present coming of the kingdom of God we are (in some measure) enabled to pass through the flaming sword into paradise of God and live in righted erotic relations.*

---

* The qualifier "in some measure" is a recognition of the complexity and tragedy of the human situation. Though the kingdom of God is "already here," it is also "not yet." Though in many areas of life we have experienced the redemptive touch of God, other areas remain untouched, and we must live in anticipation of the continuing "salvation of the Lord." This is as true in our sexuality as it is in every other area of life.

In Christ we affirm our full sexuality and, through the power of the gospel, turn away from its perversion.

LOVE CELEBRATED

If Genesis affirms our sexuality, the Song of Solomon celebrates it. Karl Barth has called the Song of Solomon an expanded commentary upon Genesis 2:25—"And the man and his wife were both naked, and were not ashamed." And indeed it is! There is nothing else in our Bible that quite compares with its lavish celebration of human sexuality. That it is in Scripture at all is an elegant testimony to the Hebrew refusal to chop life into things sacred and things secular.

What a beautiful window the Song of Solomon is into eros as it should be! There is sensuality without licentiousness, passion without promiscuity, love without lust. Let me lift up four great themes in this book.

The first is love's intensity. The singer goes to great lengths, piling superlative upon superlative, to show the extravagance of their love. "Sustain me with raisins, refresh me with apples; for I am sick with love," cries the woman (Song of Sol. 2:5).

At another point the singer describes the woman in bed longing for her lover. She gets up in the middle of the night and roams the deserted streets looking for "him whom my soul loves" (3:2). She even accosts the watchmen, pleading for knowledge of her lover's whereabouts. Finally, "I found him whom my soul loves. I held him, and would not let him go" (3:4), a beautiful opening onto love's intensity. It is, indeed, eros without shame.

Alongside love's intensity we need to see love's restraint. There is no crude orgy here, no pawing and pounding. Love is too high, sex is too deep, for such leering and lusting.

In chapter 8 the woman remembers what her brothers said of her when she was a child. "We have a little sister, and she has no breasts." (That is, she has not yet matured.) "What shall we do for our sister, on the day when she is spoken for? If she is a wall, we will build upon her a battlement of silver; but if she is a door, we will enclose her with boards of cedar" (8:8-9). In essence, the brothers protectively ask, "Was our sister a wall? Did she keep herself pure? Did she keep her erotic passions in control, reserving herself for her loyal, permanent lover? Or was she a door? Was she violated by temporary lovers?"

Fully matured, the woman gladly announces to her lover, "I was a wall, and my breasts were like towers" (8:10). She had not given in to unrestrained passion.

The man, too, knew the lessons of restraint. In chapter 6 he recalls the numerous opportunities he could have had to show his sexual prowess. In what is perhaps a bit of Hebrew hyperbole he mentions sixty queens, eighty concubines, and "maidens without number" that could have been his, yet he said no to them all, for "I am my beloved's and my beloved is mine" (6:3, 8).

Love in the Song of Solomon is restrained also in that it refuses to be rushed. This is captured well by the chorus that threads its way through the book: "I adjure you, O daughter of Jerusalem . . . that you stir not up nor awaken love until it please" (3:5; 5:8; 8:4). And if it was important for ancient Israel to hear that counsel of patience and restraint, how much more important for our society, which takes even children and makes them sex symbols.

Such a beautiful combination—this intensity and restraint. Erotic passion is celebrated, but it also has an exclusive character. No passage illustrates this better than the wedding scene. The man describes his bride-to-be as "a garden locked, a fountain sealed" (4:12). She has said no to capricious sex; she has kept her garden locked. But then we come to the wedding night, when the woman calls out: "Awake, O north wind, and come, O south wind! Blow upon my garden, let its fragrance be wafted abroad. Let my beloved come to his garden, and eat its choicest fruits" (4:16). Love's intensity. Love's restraint.

A third theme that weaves its way through the Song of Solomon is love's mutuality. Nowhere in this book do you find the dull story of the man acting and the woman being acted upon—quite the contrary! Both are intensely involved; both initiate; both receive. It is as if the curse of man's domination that resulted from the fall has been surmounted by the grace of God.

Even the literary structure of the book emphasizes that love is reciprocal. The man speaks; the woman speaks; the chorus sings the refrain. There is open-hearted dialogue. The woman is open and unashamed in her expressions of love and passion: "My beloved is a sachet of myrrh lying between my breasts," "My beloved is like a gazelle, like a young stag" (1:13; 2:9, Jerusalem Bible).

In Genesis we are told only of Adam's attraction to Eve, but here the accent is upon the lovers' mutual attraction. Both are constantly giving and receiving in the act of love, love's mutuality.

The final theme we should see is love's permanence—no promiscuity here, no running away when bills and boredom set in. Toward the end of the Song the woman cries out:

> Set me as a seal upon your heart,
> as a seal upon your arm;
> for love is strong as death,
> jealousy is cruel as the grave.

Its flashes are flashes of fire,
a most vehement flame.
Many waters cannot quench love,
neither can floods drown it.
If a man offered for love
all the wealth of his house,
it would be utterly scorned. (8:6-7)

Their love is ongoing and strong. It transcends the hot-cold fluctuations of erotic passion. It is as strong as death; it cannot be bought at any price. Indeed, these words of fidelity and permanence remind us of the love-hymn of the apostle Paul in 1 Corinthians 13—"Love never ends."

How telling is this word of love's permanence! David Hubbard comments, "The loyalty pictured in the Song should remind [us] that there's no way out of this. There's no rip cord that can be pulled, no ejection seat that can be triggered. They are in it together, bound to each other forever with covenantal loyalty."[3]

Love's intensity, love's restraint, love's mutuality, love's permanence—all marvelous windows onto human sexuality.

JESUS AND SEXUALITY

We now turn our attention to Jesus' own affirmative attitude toward sexuality. Actually, we have very little direct teaching from Jesus on sexuality, no doubt primarily because his teachings were in organic unity with the Old Testament's insights and he felt no need to elaborate further upon them. However, what we do have underscores Jesus' high view of sex and of marriage.

Jesus had a high view of sex. The Scribes and Pharisees taught that as long as you stayed away from adultery you were okay. But Jesus saw beyond the externalities of law to the internal spirit in which people live. "I say to you that every one who looks at a woman lustfully has already committed adultery with her in his heart" (Matt. 5:28).

Lust produces bad sex, because it denies relationship. Lust turns the other person into an object, a thing, a nonperson. Jesus condemned lust because it cheapened sex, it made sex less than it was created to be. For Jesus, sex was too good, too high, too holy, to be thrown away by cheap thoughts.

Jesus also evidenced a high view of marriage.* In Matthew 19 we see the Pharisees attempting to trap him by embroiling him in the raging debate of the day about the grounds for divorce. Jesus responded by appealing to the "one flesh" teaching of the creation narrative, adding, "So they are no longer two but one. What therefore God has joined together, let no man put asunder" (Matt. 19:6). In these words of Jesus we are confronted with the great mystery of the life-uniting reality of "one flesh." There is a merger of two that, without destroying individuality, produces unity. The two become one flesh! What a wonder! What a mystery! It is a spiritual reality that we will want to look at again and again.

PAUL AND SEXUALITY

The apostle Paul likewise honored marriage, by comparing it to the covenant relationship between Christ and his Church. After quoting the Genesis passage about the husband leaving father and mother and cleaving to his wife so that the two become one flesh, Paul adds, "This is

---

* Jesus gave a valid place for the single life, too. We will look at this aspect of his teaching in Chapter 7.

a great mystery, and I take it to mean Christ and the church" (Eph. 5:32).

To be sure, Paul spoke with favor and zeal about the value of the single life (1 Cor. 7). But even there, he affirmed marriage and counseled mutual sexual fulfillment, "The husband should give to his wife her conjugal rights, and likewise the wife to her husband" (1 Cor. 7:3).

What have we seen in this brief biblical overview? From the Old Testament to the New Testament, from the Gospels to the Epistles, we have heard the call to celebrate our sexuality. Our sexuality is intimately tied to who we are as spiritual persons. The spiritual life enhances our sexuality and gives it direction. Our sexuality gives an earthy wholeness to our spirituality. Our spirituality and our sexuality come into a working harmony in the life of the kingdom of God. So runs the witness of the Bible.

THE JUDGMENT OF HISTORY

I wish I could speak as warmly about the witness of the Church through the centuries. Two major departures from the biblical perspective began to develop soon after the apostolic age. The first is the view that physical pleasure is bad, and the second is that sexual intercourse should be reserved for procreation. Sexual pleasure began to be looked upon as the enemy of the spiritual life.

Perhaps no one did more to bring these teachings into the heart of the Church than Saint Augustine. No doubt his own sexual escapades as a youth help to account for his negative attitude toward sexuality after his conversion. In *The City of God*, he refers to "the shame which attends all sexual intercourse."[4]

Even within marriage he saw sexual intercourse, except for the sake of begetting children, to be venial sin. Of his influence in these matters, Derrick Bailey has noted,

"Augustine must bear no small measure of responsibility for the insinuation into our culture of the idea, still widely current, that Christianity regards sexuality as something peculiarly tainted with evil."[5]

Many theologians, however, went even further than Augustine. Some warned couples that the Holy Spirit left the bedroom whenever they engaged in sexual intercourse. One Yves of Chartres counseled the devout to abstain from sexual intercourse on Thursdays in remembrance of Christ's rapture, on Fridays in remembrance of Christ's crucifixion, on Saturdays in honor of the Virgin Mary, on Sundays in commemoration of Christ's resurrection, and on Mondays out of respect for departed souls.[6]

The Protestant Reformers were more accepting of human sexuality but were worried about lust in a fallen world and so urged sexual restraint both in and out of marriage. Some, however, had a more positive approach. Jeremy Taylor, in *The Rule and Exercise of Holy Living and Dying*, encouraged sexual intercourse "to lighten and ease the cares and sadnesses of household affairs, or to endear each other."[7] Contrary to popular belief, the Puritans had quite a positive and healthy perspective on sexuality. They saw sexual intercourse as essential to marriage, and it was encouraged as a gift of God. Edward Morgan, in "The Puritans and Sex," noted that "the Puritans showed none of the blind zeal or narrow-minded bigotry which is too often supposed to have been characteristic of them."[8]

Overall, however, we have to recognize that the Church has not maintained the high celebrative view of sexuality that is characteristic of the Bible. How tragic it is that the Church has often ignored the unashamed eroticism of the creation story and the sensual joy of the Song of Solomon. How sad it is that the New Testament's affirmation of sex and marriage has often been twisted into a denial of our sexuality. We must turn again to a more biblical, more Christian posture.

DISTORTED SEXUALITY

Though the Bible celebrates our sexuality, it also provides warnings.* This side of the fall, we often understand our sexuality through a glass darkly. Our task as Christians is to pick our way through sexuality's distortions and into sexuality's wholeness. Sin has distorted sexuality in many ways.

Pornography is a distortion of sexuality. That pornography cannot be defined in absolute terms should not obscure its existence. There is a world of difference between the nude figures in the Sistine Chapel and those in a "skin" magazine, and any reasonable person knows the difference. "Pornography is harmful," says Lewis Smedes, "because it makes sex trivial, uninteresting, and dull."[9] Art or literature moves closer to pornography the more it cuts off our sexuality from the full range of human activity and feeling. In pornography we see a truncated sexuality concerned only with the physical as an activity of lust and a dehumanizing exercise of power over others. Pornographic art cheapens and dehumanizes; true art lifts and ennobles.

One feature of the pornographic business is the fantasy world it creates. Staged photo sessions and the miracle of dye-transfer printing can cover a multitude of flaws. The slick film, with its carefully packaged titillations, can make an otherwise wholesome marriage relationship seem tedious and drab by comparison. What woman can

---

* The views of sexuality we have just seen in the history of the Church stem, in part at least, from a concern for taking the warnings of Scripture seriously The problem is that their exclusive attention to the warnings produced an inability to appreciate the positive, celebrative side of sexuality.

compare favorably day in and day out with the voluptuous breasts, sparkling smile, and sensuous legs seen on the screen today? What man can match the bulging biceps and suntanned body portrayed in the modern media?

The answer is that no one can, not even the people who stage the phony show. It is a dream world—a deceptive, beguiling, artificial dream world. The sex of the pornographic trade is too slick, too wonderful, too ecstatic. Sex in the real world is a mixture of tenderness and halitosis, love and fatigue, ecstasy and disappointment. When people believe the dream world, they begin to cast a disparaging eye at the flaws of the real world; indeed, they begin to seek a flawless fantasy world. Such make-believe is genuinely destructive to both true sexuality and true spirituality.

All this is destructive enough, but perhaps the most destructive aspect of pornography is the twisted forms of power it portrays. Hard-core pornography is far more than titillation; it is violent and sick. It appeals to raw power, sadistic and destructive.

Lust is also a distortion of sexuality. When I speak of lust, I am not referring to the casual glance or the fleeting thought but to a condition in which a person lives in a perpetual sexual stew. Lust is runaway, uncontrolled sexual passion.

Because of sin, our sexual appetites have been distorted. In some cases, they have become obsessive and all-consuming. C. S. Lewis graphically illustrates the twistedness of our sexual instinct: "Or take it another way. You can get a large audience together for a strip-tease act—that is, to watch a girl undress on the stage. Now suppose you came to a country where you could fill a theatre by simply bringing a covered plate on to the stage and then slowly lifting the cover so as to let every one see, just before the lights went out, that it contained a mutton chop or a bit of bacon, should you not think that in that country something had gone wrong with the appetite for food?"[10]

Lewis is right; something has gone wrong with the sexual appetite, and it is a tremendous burden for some. There is the feeling of being trapped, plagued and guilt-ridden. The pious platitudes of religion do not chase away these morbidly inflamed instincts. Frederick Buechner, an acclaimed author and Presbyterian minister, has written, "Lust is the ape that gibbers in our loins. Tame him as we will by day, he rages all the wilder in our dreams by night. Just when we think we're safe from him, he raises up his ugly head and smirks, and there's no river in the world flows cold and strong enough to strike him down. Almighty God, why dost thou deck men out with such a loathsome toy?"[11]

All of us can identify with Buechner's plaintive query. But some identify more deeply, more desperately, than others. They cry out for deliverance, but heaven seems to turn a deaf ear. They feel plagued by sexual temptation all the day and all the night. They reject adultery out of Christian conviction but feel driven to pale voyeurism to satisfy the inner craving. But rather than satisfy, it only serves to inflame the desires all the more, a little like leading a starving person past a bakery. Indulgence is followed by guilt and remorse, which is followed by more indulgence and more guilt and more remorse.

We must be slow to condemn and quick to listen to all who are plagued by lust. The temptations are great in our sex-soaked culture. The distortion of our sexuality into lust can take a very tangled, twisted route. Only by the grace of God and the loving support of the Christian fellowship can our lust-inflamed sexuality be straightened upright again.

The strange twists and quirks of sexuality sometimes wind down the paths of *sadism* and *masochism*. The sadist enjoys giving pain, and the masochist enjoys receiving it.

Both are far from the warm, mutual sexuality of the Song of Solomon. Now, I am not talking about the sexual arousal that couples experience with a hard kiss or scratch. The eccentricities of a spouse can be borne within the context of responsible loving and caring.

In sadism and masochism the movement is not toward, but away from, responsible loving and caring. The focus is upon the pain rather than the building of a relationship. Lewis Smedes has noted, "Here a person is not feeling pain *within* a sexual relationship but is experiencing pain as a *substitute* for a sexual relationship."[12]

What is it that leads human beings to enjoy giving and receiving abuse, humiliation and pain? At its extreme sadism takes the form of rape or even murder. The very thing that was created to give joy and life has been twisted and used to bring misery and death. Why? What heinous quirks of sexuality would drive a person to want to dominate and humiliate and even destroy another? No one can adequately answer such questions. We can only say that sexuality's distortions can become demonic indeed. Sin is real; evil is real; the powers and principalities are real and can lead us to the very brink of hell itself.

But we must not be quick to cast stones. Within all of us lurks the potential to dehumanize and destroy. If our temptations do not come in the form of sadism or masochism, they still come and they can still destroy. These realities should humble us beneath the cross and cause us to pray for one another that health and wholeness may abound.

Sexism is yet another distortion of our sexuality. In reality, sexism is merely another side of sadism. It is the drive to dominate, to control, to hold under one's thumb. History bears the sad record of this cruel domination, primarily by men over women. Even in the Old Testament community, women were often treated as property to be protected and disposed of at male discretion.

The notion of female inferiority is a false and soul-destroying doctrine. And if we reject the inherent inferiority of the woman, we must also reject the inherent subordination of the woman. The argument that, although the woman is not inferior to the man she is different from him and therefore necessarily subordinate to him, is not compelling. Differences are obvious, but they do not necessarily entail hierarchical arrangements.

We need to be reminded that the rule of the male *over* the female is not a description of pristine sexuality before the fall but of the curse of the fall; "Yet your desire shall be for your husband, and he shall rule over you" (Gen. 3:16). Sexism is sexuality's distortion, not its wholeness. In the power of Christ's death and resurrection, we have overcome the curse of the fall, we are overcoming the curse of the fall, and we will overcome the curse of the fall.

HOMOSEXUALITY AND THE CHRISTIAN

For many reasons, I genuinely wish I could avoid the subject of homosexuality. For one thing, anything I can say in a few short pages will be wholly inadequate. Also, heterosexuals are, by the very nature of things, terribly ignorant of the homosexual experience. This is true no matter how hard we may try to understand the homosexual milieu and no matter how much we may read in order to inform ourselves about the issues involved. And then, of course, homosexuality is so volatile a matter right now in the Christian community that whatever is said will be severely criticized—and probably for good reason. However, none of this is sufficient cause for me to remain silent, and besides, the matter of homosexuality has caused so much suffering and hurt today that if anything can be said that would be helpful—perhaps even healing —it would be well worth any risk involved.

Because this issue has wounded so many people so deeply, the first word that needs to be spoken is one of compassion and healing. Those who are clearly homosexual in their orientation often feel misunderstood, stereotyped, abused, and rejected. Those who believe that homosexuality is a clear affront to biblical norms feel betrayed by denominations that want to legislate homosexuality into church life.

There is a third group that has been hurt by the contemporary battle over homosexuality: I refer to those who agonize over their own sexual identity, those who feel torn by conflicting sexual urges and wonder if perhaps they are latent homosexuals. Perhaps this group suffers the most. They are cast into a sea of ambiguity because the Church has given an uncertain sound. On their right, they hear shrill denunciations of homosexuality, and, though they appreciate the concern for biblical fidelity, they have been offended by the brash, uninformed, pharisaical tone of the pronouncements. From their left, they hear enthusiastic acceptance of homosexuality and, though they appreciate the compassionate concern for the oppressed, they are astonished at the way the Bible is maneuvered to fit a more accommodating posture.

All who are caught in the cultural and ecclesiastical chaos over homosexuality need our compassion and understanding. We need to ask forgiveness of all homosexual persons who have been discriminated against and persecuted. We need to listen with empathy to all who feel the Church is losing its moral fiber. All who are struggling with their own sexual identity need our understanding, counsel, and sober moral judgment.

Does the Bible give us any guidance on the question of homosexuality? Yes, the Bible is quite clear and straightforward. From beginning to end it views the heterosexual union as God's intention for sexuality and sees homosexuality as a distortion of this God-given pattern. Now, this conclusion is not built simply on the specific references to homosexuality in the Bible, though these passages are, I think, clear enough in their disavowal of homosexual practice.* But it is the larger biblical context that is most persuasive. That context makes it quite clear that heterosexual union is the norm. God created them "male and female" with the intent that they should become "one flesh." That conviction undergirds all the biblical teaching about human sexuality.

Now, it is quite possible to argue that the biblical authors did not understand the distinctions between homosexual lust and homosexual love or between confirmed constitutional homosexuals and those with only inclinations toward homosexuality. But it is not really possible to say that the Bible is ambiguous about this matter. Homosexuality is rejected as "unnatural" and a departure from God's intention. The notion that homosexuality is merely a special form of normal sexuality is unthinkable from a biblical perspective.

To be clear about the Bible's assessment of homosexuality does not mean that we jump to the conclusion that it is simply self-chosen. The idea that all homosexuals freely choose the form their sexuality takes and freely choose homosexual activity is neither good science nor good theology. It is not even good sense. Homosexuality comes in many degrees and has various causes, many of them beyond the individual's control. A person with a 20 or 30 percent inclination toward homosexuality finds it much easier to be "converted" to a full heterosexual orientation than a person with an 80 or 90 percent homosexual inclination. The factors that contribute to a person's sexual orientation are often deep-seated and complex. Hence,

---

* See for example, Lev. 18:22; 20:13; Rom. 1:21–27; 1 Cor. 6:9; and 1 Tim. 1:10. I am well acquainted with the various attempts to reinterpret these passages in a new light, and some of these efforts are quite sophisticated. I do not, however, find them compelling.

though we want to confess heterosexuality as the Christian norm, we also want to empathize and stand with those who find such an orientation foreign and difficult.

Simple sexual attraction to a person of the same sex is a very different thing from homosexuality. Such attraction can be triggered by various things, acceptance, affection, and caring, for example. This is quite different from true homosexuality.

You see, a woman is not a lesbian just because she feels sexually attracted to another woman. A man is not a homosexual just because he is aroused by other men. Sexual arousal is not uncommon in a context of intimacy and affection. It is not abnormal or unusual. And in our day, when so much emphasis is placed upon sex, it is quite possible for heterosexual persons to become so obsessed with sex in general that they seek to express it in both heterosexual and homosexual ways. Such drives do, however, need positive control and redirection.

A person who has experienced same-sex arousal need not be frightened that he or she is destined for a life of homosexuality. The experience is quite common but needs to be responded to firmly and appropriately. A theological, sociological, and psychological framework is needed to help channel sexuality. That framework can be used to say a firm no to homosexual activity in much the same way that a married person uses a Christian framework to say a firm no to extramarital sexual activity.

Sex is like a great river that is rich and deep and good as long as it stays within its proper channel. The moment a river overflows its banks, it becomes destructive, and the moment sex overflows its God-given banks, it too becomes destructive. Our task is to define as clearly as possible the boundaries placed upon our sexuality and to do all within our power to direct our sexual responses into that deep, rich current.

Up to this point I have dealt with those who have

same-sex *responsiveness* but not those who have firmly established patterns of same-sex *preference.* These latter individuals we call constitutional homosexuals. Try as they might, they are simply not aroused by the opposite sex; and try as they might, they seemingly cannot avoid being aroused by the same sex. Social scientists tell us that about 5 percent of all males and about half that percentage of all females have a confirmed sexual drive toward persons of their own sex. What is to be said for those who, as best we can determine, are confirmed constitutional homosexuals?

The first thing that needs to be said is that they did not choose their homosexuality any more than a clubfooted child chose clubfootedness. Both are distortions of God's intention, but neither are blameworthy. We live in a fallen world, and many are trapped by the condition of sin that plagues the human race. Such persons deserve our understanding and empathy, not our condemnation.

But although homosexuals are not responsible for their homosexuality, they are responsible for what they do. Choices must be made, and for Christians who find themselves with a homosexual orientation, those choices must be made in the light of God's truth and God's grace.

In general there are three basic options for homosexuals: to change their homosexual orientation, to control their homosexual orientation, or to practice their homosexual orientation.

Can a constitutional homosexual develop a heterosexual orientation? This question is hotly debated. Verifiable evidence is extremely hard to find. Many of the so-called conversions to heterosexuality are probably of people with leanings toward homosexuality rather than true constitutional homosexuals. Some studies do, however, give hope. Pattison and Pattison, writing in the *American Journal of Psychiatry*, conclude, "The data provide a substantial body of evidence for the plausibility of change from exclusive homosexuality to exclusive heterosexuality, which is in accordance with the Kinsey statistical probabilities for such change, the Masters and Johnson data, and the clincial or observational anecdotes of such change."[13]

Certainly we want to avoid a naive optimism, but we should always hold high the hope of genuine permanent change. Those who work for a change in their sexual orientation need the prayerful support and love of the Christian fellowship. Their way is not easy, and we in the Christian community need to stand with them through times of frustration, discouragement, and failure. Our concern, our prayer, our hope is to bring the life-changing power of God into their situation. And every single time this occurs, we can rejoice with those who rejoice. But we must also be prepared to weep with those who weep.

There are those who have cried out to God and done everything they know to do and yet have experienced no change in their sexual orientation. We who work with them have also done everything we know to do but to all appearances have failed. What happens then? A second option is to control homosexual behavior. Faced with their homosexuality, some have chosen celibacy as the route of moral integrity. These individuals need our warmest support and encouragement. Behavior modification, personal discipline, and wise judgment will be needed. The church community should surround such persons with earnest prayer that they can be faithful to their calling of celibacy.*

The third option homosexuals have is to practice their homosexuality. At this point, it would be very easy to close the discussion by declaring that the practice of

---

* Celibacy is a valid calling for homosexuals, but I am not suggesting that all celibate people are homosexuals.

homosexuality is sin and therefore not an option for Christians. The practice of homosexuality is sin, to be sure, but that does not mean we can therefore wash our hands of the matter. We live in a catastrophically fallen world, and sin's distortions can at times entangle us in tragic ways. Human strength may not always permit the ideal. We are finite; there are limits to our knowledge and power. Of course, we hope for God's power to come; we pray for God's power to come; we expect God's power to come. When it does, it is a wonderful occasion for doxology. But there are other times, times of frustration and discouragement and failure, and when those times come, we must manage as best we can.

The Christian fellowship cannot give permission to practice homosexuality to those who feel unable to change their orientation or to embrace celibacy. But if such a tragic moral choice is made, the most moral context possible should be maintained.

An analogy may be helpful. If a war is entered into when it should have been avoided, there are still moral constraints upon the combatants. Just because the ideal has been violated does not mean that anything goes. A person continues to have moral responsibilities even when driven to engage in an activity that is less than the best. If we cannot condone the choice of homosexual practice, neither can we cut off the person who has made the choice. No, we stand with the person always ready to help, always ready to pick up the pieces if things fall apart, always ready to bring God's acceptance and forgiveness.

We have had two objectives in this chapter. The first was to understand the biblical vision of human sexuality. The second was to see some of the distortions of this vision so that we can know better how to bring our lives into conformity with the ways of God. We now want to turn our attention to how this vision of wholeness in sexuality works its way out in the single life.

7. Sexuality and Singleness

Hell is the only place outside heaven where we can be safe from the dangers of love.

—C. S. LEWIS

One of the great challenges for the Christian faith today is to integrate sexuality and spirituality within the context of the single life. We are fast approaching the day when single people will be in the majority. There are, of course, the young who are still anticipating marriage. Also, there are many who are unwillingly hurled into single life by the tragic death of a spouse. The even greater tragedy of divorce casts untold millions more into the world of the single.

The Church can make an enormous contribution by helping singles grapple with their sexuality with honesty and integrity. But in order to do this we must stop thinking of single persons as somehow devoid of sexual needs. Singles—especially those with a serious Christian commitment—really struggle with their sexuality. They face many troubling questions. Is masturbation a legitimate expression of sexuality for a Christian? How do I deal with the feelings of lust that often seem to dominate my thinking? What is lust, anyway, and how is it different from appropriate sexual desire? What about physical affection? Is it an appropriate means of building a healthy relationship, or is it only a one-way street to sexual intercourse? And speaking of intercourse, why is so much significance given to the insertion of the penis into the vagina? Are there really valid biblical reasons for the ban on intercourse outside of marriage, or are these just social customs? These and many similar questions are faced by all singles who are seeking to integrate their Christianity and their sexuality.

SEXUALITY AND SEXUAL INTERCOURSE

Perhaps it is best to begin by seeking to grasp a Christian perspective on sexuality and sexual intercourse. Sometimes a person will ask, "Do you believe in premarital sex?" The answer to that question is, "yes and no." Christianity says a clear yes to that question insofar as it refers to the affirming of our sexuality as human beings. Christianity says a clear no to that question insofar as it refers to genital sex. Let us try to understand the reasoning behind both the yes and the no.

We are sexual persons. We must never try to deny or reject that in any way. We are created in the image of God, male and female. In an important sense all that we are and all that we do has sexual implications. I am trying here to overcome the really silly notion that single persons are somehow asexual.

The single person's sexuality is expressed in his or her capacity to love and to be loved. Not all experiences of intimacy should eventuate in marriage or in genital sex. Loving does not need to be genital to be intimate, and the capacity to love is vital to our sexuality. And so the single person should develop many relationships that are wholesome and caring. Deeply affectionate but nongenital relationships are completely possible and should be encouraged.

The single person's sexuality is expressed in the need to experience emotional fulfillment. The decision to reserve genital sex for marriage is not a decision to remain emotionally unfulfilled. Warm, satisfying friendships are legitimate ways single people can express their sexuality. Emotional fulfillment is completely possible for the single person, and the Church can help here by providing a context for happy and satisfying friendships to develop.

The single person's sexuality is expressed in learning to accept and control his or her sexual feelings. Individuals outside the covenant of marriage should not deny or repress their sexual feelings. Donald Goergen has noted that "feelings are meant to be felt, and sexual feelings are no exception."[1] When we try to deny these feelings we cut ourselves off from our humanity.

I hear a lot more talk about platonic love than I see in experience. Most intimate heterosexual friendships have erotic dimensions to them. And it does us no good to deny that fact of life. Rather we should accept these feelings. But to accept them does not mean to act upon them. Sexual feelings are not to control us; we are to control them. It is an illusion to think that sexual desires are uncontrollable. Just because we may feel angry enough to want to murder someone does not mean that we will do so. We control our feelings of anger so that we do not kill, and in the same way we bring our sexual feelings under our authority.

So far we have tried to show ways by which singles should say yes to their sexuality. What about the no side of the answer to the question of sex outside of marriage?

There is no getting around it: biblical teaching places a clear veto on sexual intercourse for single people. The question is, Why? The biblical writers were not in the least prudish about sex. God's very creation of human beings as male and female suggests a wholehearted approval of exciting sexual experience. The Song of Solomon celebrates sex as a voluptuous adventure. Paul warns spouses against withholding "conjugal rights." Why, then, would sexual intercourse be reserved for the covenant of marriage?

The Bible's ban on sexual intercourse for the unmarried is based upon a profound positive insight. According to the biblical authors, sexual intercourse creates a mysterious, unique "one flesh" bond. In the creation narrative we are told in simple, yet profound, words, "Therefore a man leaves his father and his mother and cleaves to his wife, and they become one flesh" (Gen. 2:24). When the Pharisees sought to embroil Jesus in the contemporary controversy over the grounds for divorce, he appealed to the "one flesh" concept of Genesis and added, "So they are no longer two but one flesh. What therefore God has joined together, let no man put asunder" (Matt. 19:6). In Ephesians, Paul quotes the "one flesh" account to urge husbands to love their wives, because "he who loves his wife loves himself" (Eph. 5:28). His point is a simple one: marriage creates such a bonded union that to do violence to one's spouse is to do violence to oneself.

For our purposes, however, the most graphic passage of all is found in Paul's teaching in 1 Corinthians 6. Paul is dealing with the case of a man in the Christian fellowship who had been involved with a prostitute. He writes: "Do you not know that he who joins himself to a prostitute becomes one body with her? For, as it is written, 'The two shall become one flesh' " (1 Cor. 6:16). This passage makes it unmistakably clear that Paul sees sexual intercourse as the act par excellence that produces a "one flesh" bond.

We are now in a position to see why biblical morality reserves sex for the covenant of marriage. Sexual intercourse involves something far more than just the physical, more than even the emotions and psyche. It touches deep into the spirit of each person and produces a profound union that the biblical writers call "one flesh." Remember, we do not *have* a body, we *are* a body; we do not *have* a spirit, we *are* a spirit. What touches the body deeply touches the spirit as well.

Sexual intercourse is a "life-uniting act," as Lewis Smedes calls it.[2] And Derrick Baily has added, "Sexual intercourse is an act of the whole self which affects the whole self; it is a personal encounter between man and woman in which each does something to the other, for good or for ill, which can never be obliterated. This remains true even when they are ignorant of the radical character of their act."[3]

Thus the reasoning behind the biblical prohibition of sexual intercourse for the unmarried goes beyond the common practical concerns of pregnancy or veneral disease or whatever. Genital sex outside of marriage is wrong "because it violates the inner reality of the act; it is wrong because unmarried people thereby engage in a life-uniting act without a life-uniting intent.... Intercourse signs and seals—and maybe even delivers—a life-union; and life-union means marriage."[4]

Therefore, Paul is saying no to sexual intercourse outside of marriage because it does violence to the very nature of the act itself. The act draws us into the profound mystery of a "one flesh" reality. It unites and bonds in a deep and wonderful way, wonderful, that is, when it is linked to a covenant of permanence and fidelity. When it is not, it becomes "a hollow, ephemeral, diabolical parody of marriage which works disintegration in the personality and leaves behind a deeply-seated sense of frustration and dissatisfaction—though this may never be brought to the surface of consciousness and realized."[5]

The Hebrew word for intercourse means "to know." The biblical writers understood that in sexual intercourse a special kind of knowledge was conveyed, a special kind of intimacy came into being. This reality they called "one flesh." This then is why the Bible reserves sexual intercourse for the covenant of marriage.

Where does this leave those who have engaged in intercourse outside of marriage but who now recognize that what they have done is really and truly wrong? Is the bonded reality of intercourse utterly irreversible? No, it is not irreversible, but it does demand the healing touch of God. To engage in a life-uniting act without a life-uniting intent wounds the inner spirit. Such wounds often fester and become infected so that they poison the entire spiritual life. At best, they leave ugly scar tissue.

But the wonderful news is that healing is possible. The grace of God can flow into the wounded spirit, healing and restoring. Sometimes, however, individuals are not able to do this by themselves. In such cases it is best for them to seek out a wise and compassionate physician of the soul—someone who is experienced in spiritual direction and healing prayer—who can pray for them and set them free.

In whatever way it is done, healing prayer does need to be given. We cannot just pretend that the affair never happened, no matter how casual it was. If it is not dealt with and healed, it will surface sooner or later. A friend of mine once counseled a 78-year-old woman. She had been a missionary for fifty years, but now her life, it seemed, was in shambles. She had fears day and night. She was afraid of crowds; she was afraid of stairs; she was afraid of everything. And she was depressed; a deep sadness hung over her entire life. So total was her misery that she was preparing to have shock treatments.

My friend, who is very wise in the care of souls, asked if she had been happy as a child. "Oh, yes!," she responded. The next question was a simple one, "When did you begin to feel this sadness and depression?" The reply was quick, "When I was sixteen." And so my friend asked, "Why? What happened when you were sixteen that caused the sadness?" For the first time in her life, this woman admitted that at sixteen she had had an affair with a young man. Fortunately she did not become pregnant, and the young man soon went away, but she had carried this deep wound in her spirit for over sixty years.

My friend prayed for the inner healing of this dear

woman, and, wonderfully, within a matter of weeks, the
fears and depression began to disappear, so that, as she
put it, "I am able to remember that I used to be afraid and
depressed, but I can no longer remember what it felt
like!"

This ministry of forgiving and healing through the
power of Christ is the common property of the people of
God. We can bring so much help, so much healing, if we
are willing. It is a gracious ministry that needs to abound
in the fellowship of the faithful.

SEXUAL FANTASY

Jesus, of course, made it abundantly clear that sexual
righteousness was a far deeper issue than merely avoiding sex outside of marriage. He went right to the heart of
the matter by speaking of the adultery of the heart,
"Every one who looks at a woman lustfully has already
committed adultery with her in his heart" (Matt. 5:28).
This statement was a profound advance over the external
righteousness of the scribes and Pharisees. It has also
caused a great deal of concern and confusion about sexual
fantasies.

The single person who genuinely wants to be a disciple of Christ and who therefore reserves sexual intercourse for the covenant of marriage is often confused
about how to deal with sexual fantasies. Sexual fantasies
delight—they also trouble and disturb. And the confusion
they cause is only heightened by the ambivalence of the
Christian community. When singles turn to the Church
for direction, they are usually met with either stony silence or the counsels of repression. Now, silence is no
counsel, and repression is bad counsel. Desperate, however, they try to repress their sexual feelings, but their
efforts always end in disappointment. The result is guilt,
followed by bitterness and disillusionment. The need is

great for solid practical guidance on how to deal with sexual fantasies.

At the outset we must make as clear a distinction as possible between lust and sexual fantasy. I say "as clear a distinction as possible" because we simply must admit that the lines that divide the two are sometimes shrouded in ethical mists and fogs. Although all lust involves sexual fantasy, not all sexual fantasies lead to lust. How do we know the difference?

In chapter 6 I defined lust as "runaway, uncontrolled sexual passion." Lewis Smedes has articulated the difference between the two quite well: "When the sense of excitement conceives a plan to use a person, when attraction turns into scheme, we have crossed beyond erotic excitement into spiritual adultery."[6] Lust is an untamed, inordinate sexual passion to possess, and this is a very different thing from the usual erotic awareness experienced in sexual fantasy.

Hence, the first thing that believers should do is to refuse to bear the heavy burden of self-condemnation for every erotic image that floats through their minds. Sometimes sexual fantasies signify a longing for intimacy; at other times, they express attraction toward a beautiful and winsome person. Sexual fantasies can mean many things, and we must not automatically identify them with lust.

It is also helpful to recognize the positive function of fantasy. Through fantasy we are able to hold reality at bay while we allow the imagination to roam freely. Mature people are able to utilize the imagination without ever losing touch with the real world. Some of the world's finest music and greatest inventions have come in this way.

Certainly one of the distinguishing characteristics of our human sexuality, as opposed to the rest of the creation, is our ability to reflect upon our sexuality. We can write love letters, remember the warm kiss many times over, and anticipate love's tender moments yet to come. These are sexual events, erotic experiences, and they should not be classified as lust. In fact, in marriage sexual fantasy is vitally important in awakening sexual expression. Perhaps one reason many couples are bored with sex is atrophy of their imagination.

But if sexual fantasy has its positive side, it also has its destructive side. It can be a substitute for warm friendships, which carry with them the demands and disappointments of real life. It can lead to obsession with the sexual. It can easily become a truncated preoccupation with the physical. It can be a prelude to illicit behavior.

The problem of sexual fantasies is genuinely intensified in our day because of the modern media blitz. It is virtually impossible to get away from the media's constant appeal to our sexual fantasies. Advertisers know well the power of sexual fantasy and constantly exploit that power.

However, we need to realize the authority we can have over our sexual fantasies. The imagination can be disciplined. In our better moments we can choose to place our minds on true and honorable and just and pure and lovely and gracious things. And even in our bad moments we can confess with Paul, "It is no longer I that do it, but sin which dwells within me," and know that a deeper experience of obedience is coming (Rom. 7:17).

You see, when bad people do evil they do exactly what they want to do. But when people who are seeking to follow Jesus Christ do evil they are doing precisely what they do not want to do. As Paul put it, "I do not do what I want, but I do the very thing I hate" (Rom. 7:15). When we are faced with such a condition, we say by faith, "That is not me doing it; it is sin in me, and by the grace of God and in the timing of God I shall be rid of it."

One of the most healing ministries we can render to

each other is to learn to pray for one another about our sexual fantasies. In this realm I have a friend who prays for me and I for him. The sharing is confidential, of course. The praying is spiced with laughter and joy, for it is a happy ministry to which we are called. We pray that we will be protected from sexual influences that will be destructive and harmful. We pray that Christ will enter our sexual fantasies and fill them with his light. We pray that our sexuality will be whole and full and pure. It is a gracious, wholesome, happy ministry, and I would commend it to you.

MASTURBATION

Masturbation is so closely related to the issue of sexual fantasy that it deserves attention at this juncture. Ethical judgments about masturbation run all the way from viewing it as a sin more serious than fornication, adultery, or rape to placing it in the same category as head scratching.*

One thing that is certainly uncontested is the almost universal experience of masturbation. James McCary, author of *Human Sexuality*, has found that about 95 percent

---

* In the Middle Ages the Roman Catholic church stressed the evils of masturbation because of its distance from procreation, which was thought to be the only function of sex, and even the most recent Vatican statement on the subject declares that "masturbation is an intrinsically and seriously disordered act." And in the Evangelical Protestant wing of the Church, Erwin Lutzer, in *Living with Your Passions*, comes very close to a direct identification of masturbation with sin. By contrast, most in the medical profession today regard it as normal and not harmful. James Dobson, in his popular "Focus on the Family" film series, accepts it as a normal part of growing up unless it becomes excessive. Charlie Shedd, in *The Stork Is Dead*, speaks of it as "a gift from God," since it can help to avoid promiscuous sex. The comparison of masturbation with head scratching comes from James McCary, in *Human Sexuality*, 3d ed. (New York: D. Van Nostrand, 1978), pp. 293-94.

of men and between 50 and 90 percent of women masturbate.[7] It has been said that "no other form of sexual activity has been more frequently discussed, more roundly condemned, and more universally practiced, than masturbation."[8] Nearly all adolescents masturbate and many adults masturbate from time to time throughout their lives.

The issue of masturbation is particularly acute for single people who, out of Christian conviction, have said no to sexual intercourse outside of marriage. Many important questions surface: Is masturbation a morally acceptable activity for a disciple of Christ? Even more, could it be a "gift from God," as some have suggested, to help us avoid promiscuous sex? What about the sexual fantasies that invariably crowd into the landscape of masturbation?

These questions—and many more—are of concern to all believers, but they are especially urgent to singles. Deeply concerned to do what is right, many singles find their experiences of masturbation plagued by guilt, defeat, and self-hatred. They determine never to do it again. But they do. And the pit of self-condemnation deepens.

Let us begin with a couple of indisputable facts. First, masturbation is not physically harmful in any way. On this, all medical experts agree. The old myths that masturbation will cause everything from pimples to insanity are just that—myths.

Second, the Bible nowhere deals directly with masturbation. There are no injunctions against it, as there are against homosexuality, for example. The Bible's silence on masturbation is not because it was unknown, since there are references to it in the Egyptian literature of the period. It certainly is not because the Bible is squeamish about sexually explicit topics. Now, the Bible's silence does not mean that masturbation is not a moral issue, but it does mean that any biblical help we receive will be indirect rather than direct.

Three concerns heighten the moral question of masturbation. The first is its connection with sexual fantasies. Masturbation simply does not occur in an imageless void. And many are deeply distressed by the images that do come, feeling that they qualify as the lust of the heart that Jesus spoke against (Matt. 5:28).

The second concern relates to masturbation's tendency to become obsessive. People who masturbate can become compulsive in it. They feel trapped; the practice becomes an uncontrollable habit that dominates everything. Perhaps the most distressing aspect of this obsessive process is the sense of being undisciplined and out of control.

The third concern has to do with masturbation's depersonalization. Masturbation is sexual solitaire. True sexuality leads us to a deep personal relationship with another, but masturbation is "sex on a desert island," to use the phrase of John White.

On the positive end of the spectrum, masturbation does help compensate for the uneven development that many adolescents experience in their physical, emotional, and social maturation. Many teenagers are physically ready for sex far sooner than they are for social intimacy and the responsibilities of marriage. Masturbation provides a natural "safety valve" while nature is synchronizing growth in the various aspects of life.

For married couples, masturbation can often be a mutually enriching experience when done together. Within the context of married lovemaking, it has been called "an exciting excursion into shared pleasure."[9] In fact, some couples find mutual masturbation a crucial element in the development of their full sexual potential.

What should we say to all this? Well, the first thing we should say is that masturbation is not inherently wrong or sinful. In the main, it is a common experience for most people and should be accepted as a normal part of life.

The second thing we can emphasize is its value in providing a potentially healthy genital outlet when sexual intercourse is not possible. We simply must not lay impossible moral burdens upon people, especially when we have no specific biblical teaching against masturbation. Many honest folk, told of the evils of masturbation, have prayed desperately to be set free, and in reality have been expecting God to take away their sexual desires. These expectations are completely unrealistic, and, in fact, if God were to oblige, he would be doing violence to his own creation. Sexual desire is good and needs to be affirmed, not denied.

But sexual desire also needs to be controlled, which leads us to a third affirmation: the more masturbation tends toward obsession, the more it tends toward idolatry. God is our only legitimate obsession. The body needs to be under our discipline; this is true whether we are talking about sloth, gluttony, or masturbation. The uncontrolled practice of masturbation undermines our confidence and self-esteem. Obsessive masturbation is spiritually dangerous. But we must also be aware of the opposite obsession—the obsession to quit. This obsession is especially painful because one failure can cast a person into despair. It becomes a desperate, all-or-nothing situation. And this is sad, because it is really unnecessary. We do not need to put people into impossible either/or binds. What we are after is control, balance, perspective.

Closely tied to this is a fourth affirmation: masturbation's sexual fantasies are a very real part of human life that needs to be disciplined, not eliminated. Erotic imaginings will come; the real ethical question is how to deal with them. Will they dominate every waking moment, or can they be brought into proper perspective within the far greater matters of love and human relationship? We like fantasies because they idealize life. In our fantasies we are the paradigm of sexual prowess, our partner is desirable beyond compare, and, best of all, he or she says what we want, does what we want, and never makes demands on our time and energy. This is precisely why fantasies need discipline: they can divorce us from the real world of human imperfection. And Jesus' word about adultery of the heart must never be taken lightly.

The final thing we should say about masturbation is that, although it may electrify, it can never fully satisfy. Orgasm is only a small part of a much larger whole. And that larger whole encompasses the entire range of personal human relationship. A cup of coffee together in the morning, a quiet talk in the evening, a touch, a kiss—this is the stuff of our sexuality. Masturbation will always fall short, because it seeks to perpetuate the myth of the self-contained lover.

PASSION UNDER CONTROL

Most cultures in the history of the world have not known the many expressions of courting that are so familiar to us. Marriages were arranged. Abraham sent his servant to find a bride for Isaac, and the choice was made before Isaac and Rebekah ever set eyes on each other (Gen. 24). And so it has been in many cultures. Love and intimacy came after marriage rather than before it. But this is not how it for us, not in our culture. For us, there are elaborate rituals of acquaintanceship and courtship. Many of these rituals seem innocent enough—talking together, holding hands, kissing. Others seem dangerously erotic—necking, caressing, petting.

These rituals hold no moral dilemma for those who allow sexual intercourse to run free. For them, these things can be a prelude to intercourse if the conditions are right and all things work out well. But for those who reserve genital sex exclusively for the covenant of marriage, these matters are filled with moral consequence. It is to these people that the counsel that follows is addressed.

The first question that must be answered is whether or

not there is any place at all within the context of Christian sexual behavior for the many expressions of love and affection. I am going to answer yes to that question, but first let us see why many people, to one degree or another, have tended to answer no. The main reason for a no answer is that the kissing and hugging are considered the first steps toward sexual intercourse, a process that, once begun, cannot be stopped. Now, if that is the sole purpose of these rituals of acquaintanceship and courtship, then it makes all the sense in the world to put up plenty of stop signs and barriers.

However, it is possible for the many acts of affection that accompany courtship to have an altogether different agenda. They can also serve the purpose of tender caring and sharing, of mutual endearment and intimacy. They can be enjoyed for their own sake without necessarily leading to sexual intercourse.

The purpose of the many acts of mutual affection should be to convey closeness without sexual intercourse as the goal. Singles need to understand this purpose with absolute clarity, because the pressure of society and the pressure of friends and the pressure of body chemistry will all push toward intercourse.

I am suggesting that, instead of denying our passions, we need to control our passions. Obviously, there are very real risks. Sexual passion is very powerful, and it can easily carry people beyond the point of no return before they know it. This gives rise to a second major question, If we accept the acts of mutual affection within the context of Christian ethics, are there any guidelines for their practice? These acts can range from simple hugging and kissing all the way to direct stimulation of the breasts and the genitals. What counsel can be given that might help singles find their way along this continuum?

Responsible passion should be guided by one basic principle: *increased physical intimacy in a relationship should always be matched by increased commitment to that relationship.* A diagram[10] might help illustrate this principle:

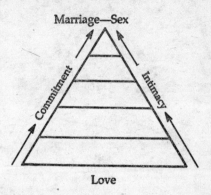

We build a solid foundation for love by moving toward commitment at the same rate we move toward physical intimacy. As intimacy grows, so does our commitment to each other. As our commitment grows, so does our intimacy. If our mutual commitment is shaky, we had better ease up on the intimacy. The early stages of commitment include such things as exclusively dating one person. Deeper levels of commitment involve such things as engagement. All along the way the privileges of growing intimacy carry with them the responsibilities of growing commitment, so that the ultimate intimacy in sexual intercourse coincides with the ultimate commitment in the covenant of marriage.

The diagram on the following page illustrates what happens when intimacy runs ahead of commitment. When people move one inch toward commitment and a mile toward intimacy, everything is thrown off balance. There is no solid foundation for love, and the result is frustration and chaos.

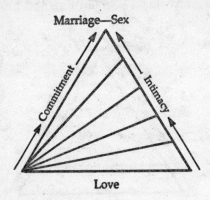

I have sought to present a general principle for responsible passion that I hope will provide guidance without legalism. I would like to add to this two opinions of my own: if these are helpful, good; if not, forget them, for they are certainly not essential to the general principle.

My first suggestion is this: since our purpose is to convey personal closeness and sharing without sexual intercourse, I think it would be wise to make the genitals and the woman's breasts off limits until marriage. These areas are just too explosive to be part of a mutual expression of affection and caring short of intercourse.

My second suggestion is that the engagement period not be too long—certainly not more than six months. By the time a couple reaches the point of engagement, they are entering levels of intimacy that should not be sustained for long without expression in sexual intercourse. For Carolynn and me the engagement period, while in many ways very wonderful, was in other ways the most difficult. Our love for each other, our caring, our sharing, was at an apex. We have always been glad that we waited until marriage for sexual intercourse, but we were also glad that the final waiting period was not unduly long.

THE SINGLE LIFE

Some have a special call of God to a single life, as both Jesus and Paul taught. This was a genuine contribution, since before this time there was no theology of sexuality that really allowed for the single life.*

Jesus declared that there were those who were single "for the sake of the kingdom of heaven" (Matt. 19:12) †
And Paul builds on this foundation by suggesting that the unmarried can focus their energies toward the work of God in a way that the married simply cannot (1 Cor. 7:32-35).

Some have railed at Paul for urging people to seriously consider the single life, but the truth is that his words are filled with practical wisdom. He was not against marriage —in fact his great contribution to Christian sexual theology is the way he compares the sexual union in marriage to the union of Christ and his Church. But Paul did insist that we count the cost. You see, no one should enter the covenant of marriage without realizing the immense time and energy required to make that relationship work.

---

* In the main, Judaism looked upon celibacy as an abnormal state Eunuchs, for example, were forbidden to act as priests (Lev. 21:20). The only exception I am aware of to this general rule was the Essene community of Qumran. There celibacy did exist, and Jesus was likely aware of this group since his cousin, John the Baptist, was probably involved with the Essenes.

† The biblical term is *eunuchs,* and there is considerable debate over whether this refers to a person who has never married or to a married person whose partner has left for a pagan life who does not remarry and hence is a "eunuch for the sake of the kingdom." Whichever interpretation is correct, the practical outcome is the same—the person lives a single life for the sake of the kingdom of heaven.

"The unmarried man is anxious about the affairs of the Lord, how to please the Lord; but the married man is anxious about worldly affairs, how to please his wife, and his interests are divided" (1 Cor. 7:32-34).

Therefore, in the Christian fellowship we need to make room for the "vocational celibate"—the person who has chosen a single life in order to focus his or her energies more narrowly on the service of the kingdom of God. Jesus himself is an example of this, as is Paul. Vocational celibacy is not an inferior or a superior way of life—it is simply a different calling.

In *Freedom of Simplicity* I have written, "We do people a disservice when we fail to proclaim the single life as a Christian option. Marriage is not for everyone, and we should say so."[11] Those who are called to the single life should be welcomed into the life and ministry of the church. They are not half-people or folk who somehow cannot snag a mate. They have made a positive choice of the single life for the sake of Christ and in response to the call of God. And as Heini Arnold has noted, "It is possible for everyone to find the deepest unity of heart and soul without marriage."[12]

Before concluding this section I want to speak a special word about those who are single but feel no special calling to be single. Perhaps they are widowed or divorced or have not had a chance to marry but wish they were married. The Christian community needs to have a special tenderness for these who feel shoved aside and left behind in our couple-oriented world.

In many cases their situation has arisen from circumstances completely beyond their control. For example, we tell people to marry "only in the Lord," but because of our mechanisms of evangelism and Christian nurture, we have more women than men in the Church. What are the women to do?

Or consider the plight of the divorcées in our

churches. In many cases we are not sure whether to welcome them or to ostracize them. They sense our ambivalence, and in some ways it is worse than outright rejection.

To the unwilling single I would like to speak the words of trust and hope. Do not harden your heart. God is still sovereign no matter what the frustrations of your life may indicate. He can bring about that "wonder of wonders and miracle of miracles" that Motel Kamzoil sang about in *Fiddler on the Roof*. Trust in him, do all you can yourself, and live in hope. And even if marriage does not come, you can know that his grace is sufficient even for that.

In writing this chapter I have been keenly aware that it is quite easy for me to pontificate on the conditions for sexual purity for singles from the warm confines of a satisfying marriage. To put it bluntly, I do not have to face an empty bed at night or mounting sexual frustrations during the day. But whatever our station in life, we can trust the goodness of God and learn to live in his power.

8. Sexuality and Marriage

Christianity does not depreciate marriage, it sanctifies it.
—DIETRICH BONHOEFFER

Marriage is a great gift of God. It ushers us into the strange and awesome mystery of "one flesh" in all its fullness. It is a gift to be received reverently and to be nurtured tenderly. To be sure, we must not elevate the gift of marriage above the gift of the single life, but neither should we underestimate its importance. Martin Luther declared, "Ah, dear Lord, marriage is . . . a gift of God. It is the sweetest and dearest, yes, purest life."[1]

In the Genesis account we are told that the bond of marriage is greater even than the bond of child to parent. "Therefore a man leaves his father and his mother and cleaves to his wife, and they become one flesh" (Gen. 2:24). Jesus refers to this Genesis passage and then adds, "So they are no longer two but one. What therefore God has joined together, let no man put asunder" (Matt. 19:6). And the apostle Paul elevates marriage to a place of high spirituality by declaring it to be a reflection of Christ and his Church (Eph. 5:21–32). The Bible, therefore, sees marriage as a great calling indeed. So much so, in fact, that Helmut Thielicke can speak of marriage as pre-eminently "the covenant of agape."[2]

CHRIST AND MARRIAGE

What constitutes an adequate basis for Christian marriage?[3] Couples of all ages struggle with this question. Are romantic feelings and the sense of mutual attraction enough? Certainly they are important, but they are not enough. It may surprise you to realize that the New Testament regards romantic love as such a minor factor in marriage that it does not even mention it. That does not mean that romantic love is without significance, but its significance must be brought into perspective with the larger considerations for marriage. One of the great tragedies of our day is the way people drop in and out of marriage solely on the basis of romantic love and sexual attraction. Eros is running amuck today because it is not subordinated to agape.* Sexual attraction and romantic love are good things to have in a marriage, but we cannot build a marriage upon them alone.

If not romantic love, then what does constitute a Christian basis for marriage? *The basis for getting married that conforms to the way of Christ is a regard for the well-being of ourselves and others and a regard for the advancement of the kingdom of God upon the earth.* Without question, this takes into account romantic love and sexual gratification (1 Cor. 7), both of which are God's creation and both of which are limited—limited in the sense that we cannot make a life out of them. Both sex and romance are elements to consider and may even be the deciding consideration in whether or not to marry a particular person, but they can never serve as *the* basis for marriage among those who follow Christ.

The point is that Christian marriage is far more than a private undertaking or a way to personal fulfillment. Christians contemplating marriage must consider the larger questions of vocation and calling, the good of others, and the well-being of the community of faith, and, most of all, how their marriage would advance or hinder the work of the kingdom of God.

---

* In simple terms, eros refers to romantic love and agape refers to divine love or charity.

I can well imagine that all this may sound terribly devoid of moonlight and rhapsody to you. And in one sense
it is, because the Bible rejects the romantic-novel paradigm for conjugating the verbs of marriage. Eros simply
must stand under the discipline of agape if we expect to
give strength and permanence to marriage.

On the other hand, there is plenty of room for romance and rhapsody within the Christian basis for marriage. In fact, the goodness that is in romance and sex is
available to us only within homes and communities ruled
by agape.

Marriage, you see, must be understood within the
larger context of the law of love (agape). Love, from a
biblical perspective, is a well-reasoned concern for the
well-being of all. A vital consideration in the decision to
marry is whether our well-being, the well-being of our
partner, and the well-being of others would be enhanced
by it.

Marriage must also be understood within the larger
context of discipleship. Christian marriage does not stand
outside our obedience to Christ; indeed, it is to be an
evidence of it. A vital consideration in the decision to
marry is whether a greater discipleship to Christ and a
further advancement of his kingdom will result from it.

Now, although this general principle can be helpful, it
can also cause problems. Life seldom comes so neatly
packaged. A potential marriage could enhance the well-
being of the couple and could at the same time be destructive for relatives. Who can accurately determine the
effect a marriage will have upon Christian discipleship?
And after all, aren't romantic feelings and sexual desires
at such a fever pitch for couples contemplating marriage
that all other considerations seem ludicrous?

Here is where we need the help of the Christian fellowship. We are not left to flounder on our own in these
matters. There are others who can lovingly and compas-

sionately help to bring us perspective and discernment. Besides, I have found that even the simple recognition of a larger, more Christian basis for marriage has a way of bringing romantic feelings and sexual desires into better perspective.

Please do not think I am opposed to romantic love. It is of vital importance in enhancing a marriage relationship. It may even be the deciding factor in who specifically to marry. But it is only one factor in deciding whether or not to marry, and not the most important factor at that. My plea is for a greater balance today.

MARRIAGE'S COVENANTAL CHARACTER

When we confess that Christian marriage initiates us into a "one flesh" reality, we are not being merely sentimental. The two become one functional reality a little like the way a computer disk drive and its disk form one functioning unit or the way a bow and arrow are essential to each other.

The result of this reality is the Christian confession that marriage is meant to be for life. It is to be a permanent covenant "for richer for poorer, in sickness and in health till death do us part." We will look at the matter of divorce in a moment, but for now, notice the advantage the permanence of marriage gives us.

Because of the covenant we have made, because of the "one flesh" reality we have experienced, we are able to transcend those times when romantic love cools. Romantic love will cool, you know. No one can maintain the intensity of eros forever; it is in the nature of eros to wax and wane. But as C. S. Lewis has noted, "Ceasing to be 'in love' need not mean ceasing to love."[4] When such times come (and they will come), agape disciplines and nurtures eros. Agape has the staying power that can fan the embers of eros into flame once again.

The moment we call for permanency in the covenant of marriage, we are calling for many other things to happen in concert with it. For example, we are calling for a commitment to make the marriage covenant work. Serious efforts to improve a marriage are tasks as sacred as Bible study or prayer. Indeed, to neglect a marriage relationship in favor of Bible study or prayer is sin, because it violates the covenant we have made in our marriage vows. Attention to our marriage is an act of obedience to God. It is one concrete way we can put the kingdom of God first in our lives. We are serving Christ when we are investing time and energy in the marriage relationship.

When we join in the covenant of marriage we join a lifelong communion with another person. And that communion, in all of its intimacy and mystery, will demand our most skillful efforts. We are committing ourselves to gladly give our best hours and our peak energy to this most taxing and rewarding effort.

CELEBRATION IN THE BEDROOM

Frankly, sex in marriage should be a voluptuous experience. It is a gift to celebrate, excellent in every way. We join in the celebration of the Song of Solomon:

> I come to the garden, my sister, my bride,
> I gather my myrrh with my spice,
> I eat my honeycomb with my honey,
> I drink my wine with my milk.
>
> Eat, O friends, and drink:
> drink deeply, O lovers! (Song of Sol. 5:1)

Gladly we respond to the counsel of Proverbs: "May her breasts satisfy you always" (Prov. 5:19, NIV).

Those who try to limit sex to procreation are simply ignoring the Bible. Scripture enthusiastically affirms sex within the bonds of marriage. Frequency of sex and variations of sexual technique simply are not moral issues, except in the sense of consideration for one another. In other words, married couples are free in the Lord to do whatever is mutually satisfying and contributes to the relationship. There is nothing inherently wrong with oral sex or mutual masturbation or many other ways to give pleasure to each other if they are mutually agreed upon.

There is an abundance of literature on sexual technique, so I will refrain from dealing with it in this book. It is enough to say that believers are free within marriage to explore the sexual realms of tenderness and delight that can lead them into deeper experiences of love.

I would, however, like to comment on the mutual rhythms of our sexuality. Sexual intercourse is not a given, something that somehow miraculously takes care of itself once we enter marriage. It needs nurture, tenderness, training, education and much more. When two persons enter into sexual intimacy, there must be a lot of emotional, spiritual, and physical give-and-take.

Men and women respond differently in the sexual experience, and we had better learn the differences. You can find them cataloged in any number of books. But what you cannot find is the unique differences that exist between you and your spouse. The books can only provide hints to point you in the right general direction. It is up to you to explore the unique and mysterious ways of your partner.

Women, the experts tell us, respond to sex more in terms of relationship, of caring, of sharing, than do men. But it is my God-given responsibility to learn the specific rhythms of my wife. How often, how intense, how slow, how fast, what gives pleasure, what offends—these and a thousand other things form the vocabulary of love. I must learn to read the language of her heart and soul, and she must learn to read mine.

This is the agony and the ecstasy of sexual intimacy. But we cannot avoid it even if we want to. Besides, it is the very thing that provides such infinite variety and lifelong pleasure in our sexual experience. No wonder the Creator made marriage permanent—after a lifetime we have only just begun to understand the marvelous inner clockwork of each other.

The reason many people become bored with sex is that they sever it from the mysterious, wondrous challenge of human personality uniting in one flesh. After all, if the only thing we see in sex is the insertion of a penis into a vagina, then it soon becomes wearisome indeed. But if the Christian witness to a "one flesh" reality is true, then nothing could be more wonderfully challenging.

So it is a spiritual undertaking to learn the ebb and flow of one another's sexuality. Our spiritual growth helps to enhance our sexual intimacy. Christian meditation often helps to sensitize us to the inner rhythm of each other. God, it seems, is keenly interested in helping us experience the full reality of "one flesh." In meditative prayer we are sometimes given a new insight into how to strengthen our sexual intimacy. Why not! God cares about such matters. We will become better, more sensitive lovers if we will give more attention to his guidance through listening prayer.

It was Dr. Norman Lobenz who said, "There is no better safeguard against infidelity than a vital, interesting marriage."[5] And certainly one place in marriage where we want to keep the mystery, the excitement, the fascination —the zip, zam, and zowie—is in sexual intimacy.

CHRIST AND DIVORCE

It is a thrilling thing to soar among the high and lofty peaks of marital success; it is quite another thing to descend into the valley of marital defeat. It is a little like the

valley of the shadow of death. All marriages face times of
sorrow and pain, but sometimes the sorrow seems too
heavy and the pain too great. What should believers do
when they are faced with the valley of the shadow in
marriage?

The answer to this question is hotly debated today.
Interestingly enough, it was hotly debated in Jesus' day.
In the Hebraic society of the Old Testament divorce was a
common practice, and so Moses set forth legislative
guidelines in an attempt to humanize it (Deut. 24:1-4).
But even these guidelines were fiercely debated. In Jesus'
day there was one school of rabbis, led by Rabbi Hillel,
who held that a man could divorce his wife for *any* reason. For example, if she burned the toast that morning, or
if he saw another woman that pleased him more—these
were sufficient grounds for divorce for the school of Hillel. Another group, led by Rabbi Shammai, felt that marital unfaithfulness was the only allowable grounds for a
man to divorce his wife. (You notice that divorce was a
male prerogative only—women had no say in the matter.)

The Pharisees sought to bring Jesus into this debate,
and so they asked him, "Is it lawful to divorce one's wife
for any cause?" (Matt. 19:3). The school of Hillel said yes;
the school of Shammai said no. Who would Jesus side
with? But rather than side with one group or the other,
Jesus brought them back to God's intention from the beginning, "Have you not read that he who made them
from the beginning made them male and female, and
said, 'For this reason a man shall leave his father and
mother and be joined to his wife, and the two shall
become one'? So they are no longer two but one. What
therefore God has joined together, let no man put asunder" (Matt. 19:4–6).

God's intent is for marriage to be a permanent "one
flesh" reality. But this, of course, raised the issue of the
Mosaic legislation, and so the Pharisees asked, "Why

then did Moses command one to give a certificate of divorce, and to put her away?" (Matt. 19:7). Now, please notice Jesus' answer to that question, "For your hardness of heart Moses allowed you to divorce your wives, but from the beginning it was not so" (Matt. 19:8).

Do you see what Jesus is saying? He is talking to men, and he says that Moses allowed divorce in order to protect women from hard-hearted men! It was better for the man to divorce his wife than to bash her head against a wall. But as Jesus said, divorce was not God's intent from the beginning.

Jesus opposed the divorce practices of his day for exactly the same reason that Moses first instituted a bill of divorcement—to protect the woman, who was utterly defenseless and trapped by a destructive and evil practice. There was great harm done to women in Jesus' day by divorce. The very word for divorce means literally "to throw away," and women could be thrown away by a very simple procedure that did not involve a court of law or even a religious organization. Only witnesses were involved, and they could be the husband's witnesses. No legal charges needed to be brought; it was simply a matter of handing the woman a bill of divorcement that said she was divorced for certain reasons, and those could be almost anything, from speaking out of turn to kicking the dog.

The woman was trapped in the patriarchial world of the first century. And Jesus was opposing this evil practice of throwing women away. He even said that any man who divorces his wife "makes her an adulteress" (Matt. 5:32). What he was getting at was that a woman who was thrown out into the street had only one way to make a living. She could not go out and get a job somewhere. She had only one thing to sell, and that is why prostitution was tolerated in first-century culture.

The one thing we need to see from all this is that Jesus

was not trying to set down a legalistic set of rules to determine when a divorce was allowable. The fact that in Matthew 5:32 Jesus seems to lend support to the school of Shammai about adultery as grounds for divorce does not mean that this is to be the one and only allowable basis for divorce, or even that adultery should mean divorce in every case.* He was not establishing rules at all: he was striking at the spirit in which people live with each other. And so when we study Jesus' teaching on divorce we must not look for the one or two or three things that make divorce allowable. No, we are to see to the heart of Jesus' teaching on human relationships within the context of first-century Palestine and seek to interpret those insights in the context of our world.

That is precisely what the apostle Paul did with regard to Corinthian society. The problem there was that many individuals had come into faith in Christ but had marriage partners who remained pagans. What was the status of that marriage relationship? And what should a believer do if the unbelieving spouse wanted to dissolve the marriage? If Paul had viewed Jesus' teaching legalistically, he would have had to tell Christians that they were bound to the marriage relationship unless there was adultery, since that is the one ground Jesus mentions for divorce (Matt. 5:32). But Paul did not do that. Instead, he instructed believers to stay in the marriage wherever possible. "But if the unbelieving partner desires to separate, let it be so; in such a case the brother or sister is not bound. For God has called us to peace" (1 Cor. 7:15).

What had Paul done? Had he ignored Jesus' teaching about divorce? No, not at all! He saw that the law of love

---

* See Matt. 5:32 and 19:9. But compare this with Mark 10:11 and Luke 16:18, where the same saying is given but without the exception clause about adultery. There is considerable debate over whether the exception clause in Matthew was a later addition to the text, since it seems to blunt the point of the teaching.

stood at the heart of Jesus' instruction on marriage and divorce, and he brought that central truth to bear on the Corinthian situation.

We must not turn Paul's counsel to the believers at Corinth into a new legalism, either. For example, some will teach that there are two and only two allowable grounds for divorce: adultery, because of Jesus' statement in Matthew 5:32, and desertion, because of Paul's statement in 1 Corinthians 7:15. Then if a woman comes in telling of marital rape and every other conceivable inhumanity, she is simply and grandly told that unless there is adultery or desertion she has no "biblical" basis for divorce. Such is the mentality (and the fatal weakness) of all attempts to turn the words of Jesus and Paul into a new legalism.

But if we are not given a set of rules, what guidance are we given on the question of divorce today? The first thing we can say is that God's intention from the beginning is for marriage to be a permanent "one flesh" reality. God created us male and female, and we are made to go together. We are complementaries—lifelong, permanent complementaries—and anything short of that violates God's intent.

So, although Christians may disagree on the allowable grounds for divorce, we can all agree that divorce is akin to cutting into a living organism.[6] We are not talking about dissolving a convenient partnership that has gone sour; it is more like amputating an arm or losing a lung. Divorce cuts into the heart and soul of a "one flesh" unity. It is possible to survive the operation, but let us be unmistakably clear that we are talking about radical surgery, not just minor outpatient care.

This being the case, believers need to see divorce as an absolutely last-ditch solution after every possible means of grace has been exhausted. Divorce is not something we turn to just because we are having trouble in our marriage or because we have "fallen in love" with someone else. No, Christian marriage is a "one flesh" union, a single organism, and we split it asunder only when no other option is open to us. Chuck Swindoll wisely notes, "Two processes ought never be entered into prematurely: embalming and divorce."[7]

We must not give up too soon. The Bible literally bristles with the hope of forgiven and redeemed relationships. God is vitally interested in the success of our marriages. The resources of a caring Christian community are available to us. The love and care of friends and neighbors are at our disposal. The wise counsel of professionals and the healing prayer of those skilled in spiritual direction can be ours.

But we live in a fallen world, and there are times when, despite all our efforts, the marriage enters the valley of the shadow of death. Every resource has been used. Every possible way to bring healing and wholeness has been tried. Still the marriage is immersed in destruction and bitterness. When such is the case, the law of love (agape) dictates that there should be a divorce. If, indeed, divorce is understood as a consequence of the law of love, the evil that is present in most divorces will be absent, and, indeed, few divorces will occur. But believers will make sure of their obedience to the law of love in any divorce by making God their lawyer and judge through prayer.

The basis for divorce that conforms to the way of Christ is, therefore, precisely the same as the basis for marriage. When it is clear that the continuation of the marriage is substantially more destructive than a divorce, then the marriage should end.

If, as the final, radical solution to an unbearable situation, divorce *is* chosen, it must not be the cruel "throwing away" that Jesus condemned. Provision must be made for the equitable division of property and other resources so that neither partner is left destitute. Further, we must not "throw away" one another emotionally but seek to diminish bitterness and enhance cordiality in every way possible.

Now, there are those who in faithfulness to God choose to stay in a bad marriage. Their decision is not wrong, but it is extremely difficult. They need the prayer and support of the Christian community. We are to suffer with them, to bear them up, and to pray for the inbreaking of God's life and light. Should they later choose divorce, they have not failed or done wrong, and they need our generous love and acceptance.

I want now to speak a word to those of you who are divorced and who fear that you did not work hard enough to save your marriage. When I spoke earlier of divorce as the "absolutely last-ditch solution after every possible means of grace has been exhausted," your heart probably sank. Deep down you wonder whether you turned to divorce too quickly. "Perhaps," you think, "perhaps, if I had stayed with it a little longer, if I had tried one more time, things would have turned out differently." If that describes your quandary, I want to ease your mind *and* your heart. Perhaps you *have* failed—we all fail—but God is greater than our failure. His mercy and forgiveness and acceptance cover it all. You cannot reclaim the past, but you can be set free from its dominion. Stay where you are. Bathe in his love and care. Accept his offer of forgiveness and his invitation to a hopeful tomorrow.

CHRIST AND REMARRIAGE

What "hopeful tomorrow" is there for those who are divorced? Can they or should they look forward to the possibility of remarriage? These are perplexing questions for those who sincerely want to do what is right.

For example, many are genuinely troubled by Jesus' statement in the Sermon on the Mount that "whoever marries a divorced woman commits adultery" (Matt. 5:32; see also Mark 10:11-12; Luke 16:18; and Matt. 19:9). Does this mean that remarriage is never allowed for believers? The language seems straightforward enough, yet why would Jesus make such a stringent prohibition? What was he striking at by forbidding remarriage?

Jesus was dealing with the aggressiveness of the male in the context of first-century culture. In that day a man could drop a woman or take up a woman at a whim, and Jesus was striking at this destructive attitude of male domination. That is why we need to look very carefully, for example, at Jesus' visit with the woman at the well (John 4). He notes that she had had five husbands and that the man presently living with her was not her husband. Jesus, you see, was making a statement of fact—there was no note of condemnation in his words, for the woman had had no say in those divorces. She had been "thrown away" five times, and she had become such "used property" that a man no longer needed to marry her to have her. And Jesus was condemning the callousness by which a man would marry and divorce and remarry with the same ease as he might buy and sell cattle. (In fact, in Jesus' day a good cow would bring a higher price than a woman on the open market!)

In his teaching on remarriage Jesus was calling attention to the degraded relationship that existed between a man and a woman when the woman had been previously married. And in his day it was indeed a degraded and degrading relationship. It was something that kept the woman in perpetual fear, constantly in a corner. The man had her under his power, which made it easy for him to abuse her. In first-century culture the divorced woman was viewed as a "secondhand woman," and Jesus was saying that when a man thinks of a woman as a cheap commodity he has her in a vicious relationship. And that still persists today, doesn't it? Many women live through hell in our day simply because their husbands treat them as "used women."

Jesus therefore spoke of remarriage as adultery, not because there was anything inherently wrong with it, but because of the attitude of contempt with which the man lived with the woman. He used the word "adultery" to refer to the kind of sexual relationship that is wrong and damaging. He did the same thing when he described the lust of the heart as "adultery" (Matt. 5:28). In both instances Jesus was pointing to the destruction done to the relationship and was condemning it.

What we must *not* do is to turn these perceptive words of Jesus about remarriage into another set of soul-killing laws. We would not even consider doing that with Jesus' other sayings. If we took as law his words about eyes and hands that offend us, we would all have truncated bodies (Matt. 5:29-30). None of us would even think of turning into a new legalism Jesus' instruction not to invite friends or relatives or neighbors when we give a banquet (Luke 14:12). And we should not do that with his teaching on remarriage, either. It is true that in the absolute will of God his creative intent is for marriage to be a permanent "one flesh" reality that should never be severed. But in the absolute love of God, his redemptive intent covers the brokenness of our lives and sets us free.

Therefore, the basis for remarriage that conforms to the way of Christ is precisely the same as the basis for marriage and divorce. When the persons involved would be substantially better off and the kingdom of God more effectively advanced by remarriage, then the law of love indicates that remarriage can and even should occur.

In the context of remarriage the practical problems of how to deal with sexual hurts and emotional wounds must be considered. Often these are not things that an individual can handle alone. There are reasons why marriages fail, and seldom is the failure exclusively one-sided. And even if it were one-sided, there would still be wounds that need healing. A remarriage is unwise without substantial movement toward such wholeness.

The Christian fellowship can often help. Compassionate listening and healing prayer can do much. Resources such as counseling and good books to read can also help. Most of all, we can provide a context for intimacy—a womb of compassion in which it becomes safe to feel and to care and to risk loving once again.

Where have we come? We have sought to understand our sexuality within the light of the biblical vision of wholeness. We have endeavored to see what this vision might look like for the single person. We have tried to understand the context in which marriage, divorce, and remarriage conform to the way of Christ. We are now prepared to focus all that we have learned on the vow of fidelity.

9. The Vow of Fidelity

The sex issue demands a new and vigorous response. It cannot be a negative or reactionary response; rather, it must be active, creative, positive. We need a response that bears witness to the rich, positive attitude of Scripture toward human sexuality. We need a response that is for all Christians and can be experienced in ordinary life. And we need a response that deals compassionately and forthrightly with our distortions of sexuality's God-given functions. That response is best crystallized in the vow of fidelity. All believers—whether male or female, whether single, married, divorced, widowed or remarried—are called to fidelity in their sexual relationships.

Fidelity means to affirm our sexuality in all its manifold complexity. We celebrate the fact that we are sexual beings with needs for tenderness and compassion, love and friendship. We stoutly refuse to think of ourselves in non-sexual terms. We know that to make a person sexless is to dehumanize that person, and we will not do that to ourselves or anyone else. We will be faithful to our God-created nature as sexual beings.

Fidelity means loyalty to our calling. Some are called to the single life. When that call is given by God and is confirmed in the community of faith, then the disciple of Christ can rest contented in this provision of God's grace. There is no need to fret and stew or cast about for other options. The believing community welcomes this calling and gift without casting disparaging innuendos about the failure to find a mate.

Others are called to marriage. They welcome their calling and do not begrudge the time and energy needed to fulfill it. The Church understands and seeks to enhance their efforts to cultivate a strong marriage and family. The Church refuses to frustrate these goals by proliferating meetings and commitments that separate the family unit.

Fidelity means directing genital sex into its God-given channel in the covenant of marriage. We say no to promiscuity before marriage and adultery after marriage. We scorn the modern myth that sexual prowess is validated by sexual conquest. We confess the wholeness, the fullness, of sexual expression found in a permanent "one flesh" relationship in marriage.

Fidelity means an enduring commitment to the well-being and growth of each other. We commit ourselves to our partner's wholeness and happiness. We desire that every gift, every talent, every ability be given every opportunity to blossom and flower. Husband and wife are each called to sacrifice for the advancement of the other.

Fidelity means mutuality. Our faithfulness means a refusal to lord it over one another. No power plays, no phony superiority, no artificial hierarchy.

Fidelity means honesty and transparency with each other. Our commitment is to take off our masks, to come out from behind our facades. Our sharing is no "trivial pursuit," but a willingness to speak the deep inner language of the heart.

Fidelity means to explore the interior world of the spiritual life together. We pledge ourselves to pray together, to worship together, to celebrate together. We invite our mates into the inner sanctuary of our own soul. We invite them to be witnesses to our struggles, our doubts, our breakthroughs, our growth.

THE MEANING OF FIDELITY FOR SINGLES

Human sexuality has many aspects, only one of which is genital intercourse. If single persons will nurture and cultivate the many other aspects of their sexuality, the genital needs will come into perspective.

In fact, what we call sexual needs are not really needs at all but wants. The body needs food, air, and water—without these human life cannot long survive. But no one has yet died from a lack of sexual intercourse. Many have lived quite full and satisfying lives without genital sex—including Jesus!

So sexual intercourse is a human want, not a human need, and the difference is significant. To understand this difference can be tremendously liberating for singles. They are not half people, unfulfilled and incomplete. They do not need sexual intercourse to experience wholeness in their sexuality.

The apostle Paul dealt specifically with this matter of "sexual needs" in his Epistle to the Christians at Corinth. They lived in a sexually charged environment, and some, sensing the liberty that is in the gospel, assumed that this meant total sexual freedom, including sexual relations with prostitutes. Evidently their slogan was "All things are lawful in Christ." Paul responded, " 'All things are lawful for me,' but not all things are helpful. 'All things are lawful for me,' but I will not be enslaved by anything" (1 Cor. 6:12).

The Corinthians then raised the issue of sex as a normal physical need, just like food. In other words, if sex is a natural physical appetite like the appetite for food, what is wrong with satisfying our sexual need whenever the urge arises? Paul's answer was that "food is meant for the stomach," but "the body is meant for the Lord" (1 Cor. 6:13). He went on to argue that the digestive system is temporal and biological and has meaning only in earthly existence. But the body is the temple of the Holy Spirit and is destined for resurrection and filled with eternal significance. Therefore, we should "shun immorality." Promiscuous sex is such a travesty of the "one flesh" principle that it violates the spiritual aspect of our bodies. "Do you not know that he who joins himself to a prostitute becomes one body with her? For as it is written, 'The two shall become one.' But he who is united to the Lord becomes one spirit with him" (1 Cor. 6:16–17). Paul's word to us, then, is that sexual intercourse is so filled with eternal significance that it should always be reserved for the permanency of marriage. Therefore, believers who are single will want to abstain from genital sex; at the same time, they will want to develop fully the many other aspects of their sexuality.

Intimacy is one facet of our human sexuality that singles should nurture. The giving and receiving of love is essential; in fact, people have literally died from its absence. We need to find friendships that are caring and life-giving. Loneliness is epidemic today, and many singles suffer from it because they have tended to equate intimacy with coitus. But the truth is that many intimate and affectionate relationships can be cultivated without sexual intercourse.

Singles can find intimacy with people by entering into their lives on many different levels. Sharing books, ideas, goals, conversation, and much more helps us to become intimate with one another. Friendships can be with both men and women, both single and married. People are rich tapestries, and learning the varied and intricate weave of each life can be great fun.

Closely associated with intimacy is that aspect of our sexuality that is revealed by touch. Touching, holding, stroking—these are valid aspects of our sexuality that should not necessarily be tied to genital sex. In fact, Ashley Montagu, in his book *Touching*, has noted that, "In the Western world it is highly probable that sexual activity, indeed the frenetic preoccupation with sex that characterizes Western culture, is in many cases not the expression of a sexual interest at all, but rather a search for the satisfaction of the need for contact."[1]

Singles should welcome the touch, the hug, the warm embrace. These are essential ingredients in our human sexuality, and it is not wise to cut ourselves off from them. Nonerotic touching is of growing interest to those in the healing professions. Nurses are learning how to stroke and cuddle babies; psychiatric workers are learning the power of simply holding a hand; and people like Mother Teresa of Calcutta have helped us all discover the healing power of the compassionate touch.

Older singles especially need the life-giving experience of touch. Many go for months without ever being touched by another human being. If people in the churches, for example, were to go to the older members of the fellowship and simply give them a friendly hug or a backrub, they would be astonished at the emotional boost they would be providing.

Another aspect of our sexuality is the appreciation of beauty and physical attractiveness. Many single people draw back from the natural appreciation we have for a handsome man or a beautiful woman for fear that it will lead to the lust of the heart that Jesus condemned. But that is not necessary. It is quite possible to admire beauty of face and figure without lust. We can learn to enjoy the eyes, the hair, the smile, the strength of shoulders and arms, the curve of hips and legs, without leering and lusting. They are lovely gifts from the Creator's hand. How dare we despise them!

The enjoyment of beauty does not need to be wicked; it simply needs to be controlled. And it can be. We can appreciate the lovely curve of bicep or breast without falling headlong into uncontrolled passion. Just because the

media tries to tie every attractive figure and every sensuous move to erotic sexuality does not mean that we have
to buy into such a fantasy world. As children of the light,
let us have beauty without lust and sensuousness without sensuality.

Still another aspect of our sexuality is the experience of
communication. Initially this takes the form of simply
talking about big and little things. Often it includes laughing. There are times too when it goes beyond human
speech, so that quietly sitting together becomes a profound experience of communication.

In my first pastorate there was one individual whose
home I would frequent just for conversation. We would
often sit in his study and talk over great ideas and dream
about what could be. Sometimes we would pause and
pray together; often we would laugh together. But what I
remember most are the times we would simply stop talking and sit together in profound silence. Enduring bonds
are built through such experiences of communication,
and they broaden and enhance our ability to be intimate.

Very often we in the Church place single people in a
real bind regarding their sexuality. We hang them on the
horns of a genuine dilemma: either marry, or bury your
sexuality. But that dilemma is false, and they do not need
to break it by opting for genital sex outside of marriage.
There is another option. It is possible to affirm and celebrate one's sexuality and still reserve genital sex for the
covenant of marriage.

Singles have the freedom in Christ to bring to the fore
and develop to the full sexuality's many other aspects of
intimacy and fellowship. This is the meaning of the vow
of fidelity for single people.

THE MEANING OF FIDELITY FOR THE MARRIED

Marriage that is Christian is covenantal.[2] A covenant is
a promise—a pledge of love, loyalty, and faithfulness. A

covenant involves continuity—the sense of a common future to look forward to and a history to look back on together. A covenant means belonging—a commitment to a rich and growing relationship of love and care. Let us seek, then, to flesh out the meaning of fidelity within the covenant of marriage.

First, fidelity in marriage means monogamy. We argue for monogamy and against polygamy, but not on the basis of biblical laws on the subject. In fact, some people would be surprised to realize that for every verse of Scripture we could marshal in the defense of monogamy we could find two for polygamy. No, the Christian witness to monogamy is based upon the revelation of agape that we have in Jesus Christ. The love that Christ bequeathed to us is an "existence-for-the-other-person" reality.[3] To be blunt, polygamy dehumanizes the woman.* The woman is made to be part of the herd for the pleasure of the man. Polygamy is an affront to the law of love. Even in the Old Testament, we can see some of the harmful results of such an arrangement.

This does not mean that we insist that people in polygamous situations immediately change to monogamy upon conversion. I know a bright student from Nigeria who has a wife and four lovely children. His father, however, had seven wives. Recently his father died, and by custom the seven wives reverted to the son. Now, for my friend to throw these women out would be terribly destructive, and so he has decided to keep all of them as his wives. He will be a husband to them in the sense of providing for their physical needs; however, he has told all seven that he will not be a husband to them sexually and

---

* I am aware that technically *polygamy* refers to multiple mates of either sex. (*Polyandry* means many husbands and *polygyny* means many wives.) Most people, however, think of polygamy in terms of multiple wives, and the practice of polygamy in most cultures has been in that direction.

therefore has given them freedom for sexual expression outside of marriage. If later they have a chance to marry someone else, he will give them a divorce—an "honorable discharge," if you will. These are certainly difficult decisions for a Christian caught in a polygamous culture, but I, for one, applaud his efforts.

Second, fidelity in marriage means a lifelong pledge to love and loyalty. Disciples must refuse to look for a way out of the covenant just because difficulties arise or romantic love cools. Difficulties are not a sign of a bad marriage; indeed, they often indicate health in the marriage. People who care for each other will have arguments and disagreements because they prize the relationship. If there never are any, it may be an indication that they just do not care anymore.

The disagreements and the arguments are not the problem but how we handle them. In *Letters to Karen*, Charlie Shedd has given his "Seven Official Rules for a Good Clean Fight" that have guided him and Martha throughout their marital disagreements, and I recommend them to you.[4] To this wise counsel I would add only one comment: never, but never, allow the conflict to become physically violent. Physical abuse damages the relationship far more deeply than we know. (And if one is looking for biblical grounds for divorce, certainly physical abuse should rank at the top.)

There are times when the conflict that a couple experiences seems unbearable. "Why try any longer?" they ask. We keep trying longer because the stakes are so high, the reward of success is so great! And if we value a long life together, we will believe that our marriage is worth a great deal of effort and struggle. Our love is too good a thing to lose.

Having said this, I also know that in certain situations there may come a time when the conflict not only seems unbearable, it is unbearable. In such circumstances, fideli-

ty suggests that wherever it is feasible the question of
divorce be brought before the Christian fellowship for
loving counsel and discernment. The Church is supposed
to be in the business of healing ruptured marriages, or
failing that, of healing the wounds of divorce.

No one is more keenly aware than I that many
churches simply could not handle such a delicate and
awesome responsibility. Often elders or other officially
designated leaders are so divided on the issues of divorce
and remarriage that they cannot help at all. Prejudice
often reigns and blots out spiritual insight. Many leaders
honestly feel that the business of the Church is to monitor
budgets and maintain buildings, not to be amateur marriage counselors.

Yet amazing healing can come from a loving fellowship that is allowed to put its arms around a broken and
bleeding marriage. It must be done with tenderness and
humility. There can be no arrogance, no gossip, and no
moralistic advice. The couple must feel assured that the
fellowship accepts them and stands with them in their
pain whatever the outcome. The main means of support
are sympathetic listening and empathetic prayer. Sometimes what emerges from such experiences seems almost
as real a resurrection as when Lazarus walked out of the
tomb. Not always, but sometimes!

Third, fidelity in marriage means mutual subordination out of reverence for Christ. The apostle Paul places
the principle of mutual subordination over all family relationships: "Be subject to one another out of reverence for
Christ" (Eph. 5:21). He then proceeds to explain the de-
tails of how mutual subordination is to operate within the
Christian household. It is truly amazing the responsibility
for submission that Paul places upon the male, who, after
all, stood at the top of the Hebrew patriarchial society.
Paul calls for Christly submission through sacrificial love.
First-century marriage customs did not view a woman as

a full person, much less as someone to whom sacrifical love was due.

To be sure, Paul places a special responsibility for submission upon the wife: "Wives, be subject to your husbands, as to the Lord" (Eph. 5:22). He also places a special function upon the man: "The husband is the head of the wife as Christ is the head of the church" (Eph. 5:23).* There are those who wish Paul had not put it quite that way, since so often this teaching has been twisted into a way of keeping women under the male thumb. However, we must remember that here Paul is using the teaching approach of connection that is so common in Scripture. He is connecting with where people are and moving them to where he would like them to be.†

What Paul is doing in this passage is really quite astonishing. Informed by the gospel liberty that came from the example of Christ, he makes a radical break with the authoritarian, hierarchical system of the past—"be subject to one another out of reverence for Christ." But in the next breath he connects with the tradition of the past—"wives be subject . . . for the husband is the head." Regarding

---

* There have been more recent attempts to translate *kephale* not as "head" but as "source" and therefore distance the passage from a hierarchial model for the husband-wife relationship. Also, the verb "to submit" does not appear in verse 22; it says simply "wives to your husband." Obviously the verb must be supplied from verse 21 and therefore is precisely the same kind of submission that is required of all believers. For a thoughtful study of this issue, see Berkeley and Alvera Mickelsen, "The 'Head' of the Epistles," *Christianity Today*, 20 Feb. 1981, pp. 20-23.

† Jesus, for example, used this principle of connection when he said, "Think not that I have come to abolish the law and the prophets" (Matt. 5:17). But given what he had just been teaching them they could not think anything other than that he had come to abolish the law and the prophets! So without backing down on his radical disjuncture with the past, Jesus proceeds to show how his teaching connects with the past and fulfills it. Paul is doing the same thing in the Ephesians passage.

this passage, Elizabeth Achtemeier has noted: "The passage is ingenious. It has preserved the traditional view of the male as the head of the family, but that headship is a function only, not a matter of status or superiority. The understanding of the headship and of the wife's relation to it has been radically transformed. There is no lording it over the other here, no exercise of sinful power, no room for unconcern or hostility toward the other. Instead there is only the full devotion of love, poured out for the other, in imitation of Christ's faithfulness and yearning and sacrifice for his church, and of the church's like response to him."[5]

In all honesty, I think it must be said that the apostle Paul does not rush into the arms of egalitarian marriage. But neither does he fit in the embrace of authoritarian, hierarchical marriage. Certainly his strong words of mutual subordination and mutual marital responsibility are moving his readers, and us, along a continuum from a patriarchal or authoritarian approach toward a partnership or companionship approach. And all of us must find our marriage place somewhere along this continuum.

The direction Paul is heading in all of this is most clearly seen in his famous statement of Galatians 3:28, "There is neither Jew nor Greek, there is neither slave nor free, there is neither male nor female; for you are all one in Christ Jesus." In the Jerusalem Council of Acts 15, the Church dealt with the issue of cultural religion —"neither Jew nor Greek." Over many painful centuries the Church finally dealt with the issue of chattel slavery—"neither slave nor free." We can hope and pray that in the providence of God the Church will soon be able to deal successfully with the issue of sexism—"neither male nor female."

What does all this mean to you and me in a practical sense? Well, to borrow from Paul's language, each of us must work out our own marriage style in fear and trembling (see Phil. 2:12). Disciples of Christ are free and equal in the gospel to work through the meaning of mutuality and submission. But there must be no lording it over one another and no headstrong rebellion. Tenderness, love, and mutual respect must govern all decisions. Always remember that the "one flesh" experience of "bone of my bones and flesh of my flesh" gives us a predisposition to walk through life's decisions in concert. Mutuality is one of fidelity's many facets.

Fourth, fidelity in marriage means sexual restraint outside of the marital covenant. When I speak of sexual restraint I mean two things: one, no extramarital genital sex and, two, expression of nongenital sexuality that is controlled by the good of the marriage and the well-being of the spouse.

The first statement needs little clarification. Adultery is not acceptable in any form for those who are followers of Jesus Christ. It does violence to the "one flesh" reality of the marriage covenant and damages the marriage relationship.

The second statement may need to be explained a bit more. Although "all things are lawful . . . not all things are helpful," as Paul put it (1 Cor. 6:12). In one sense, after marriage we are no longer our own, no longer free to choose and act as we please. Every choice, every act, affects our spouse and our marriage. Now, we may not like that, but it is a fact of life and we might just as well make peace with it. Our spouse and marriage are more profoundly affected for good or for ill by the way we express our sexuality than by nearly anything else in our lives.

This does *not* mean that we repress our sexuality outside marriage. Oh, no, hardly anything will damage the marriage more. We must be human; we need intimacy, touch, meaningful conversation, and much more outside the marriage bonds. Otherwise we will be asking the marriage to carry more than is reasonable for even the healthiest relationship.

But we really must be sensitive to how our actions and even our thoughts affect our marriage. For example, if I give all my emotional energy and attention to counseling and other relationships so that I come home with no emotional reserves for my wife and children, I am committing "emotional adultery." Both Carolynn and the boys need and deserve my emotional energy. If I am not giving Carolynn what she needs from me emotionally, I must make whatever changes are necessary to better fulfill the vow of fidelity.

Now Carolynn is involved in some things in which I have no interest. I discuss with friends some issues that she finds boring. That's fine. We want to give each other plenty of freedom and flexibility. But we also want to be sensitive to how our actions and activities affect each other. We need to maintain open and free communication —listening, not just to each other's words, but to feeling tones, body language, the language of the heart and of the spirit. As we listen, we are predisposed to restrain anything that would detract from the marriage. As Francis Moloney has noted,"The external restraint which love practises is often a mark of its freedom from internal limit."[6]

All of which leads to the fifth mark. Fidelity in marriage means sexual liberty within the marital covenant. Here we must truly let the liberty bells ring! When sex is in its own free, full channel of marriage, it is a rich and fulfilling adventure. At times the channel is fast and exciting, like the Colorado River. At other times it is quiet and placid, like the Mississippi. Often it is deep and strong, like the Columbia.

Paul sounded the high note of sexual liberty within marriage when he declared, "The husband should give to his wife her conjugal rights, and likewise the wife to her husband" (1 Cor. 7:3). Now, you might be thinking that that sounds a lot more like obligation than liberty, but I can tell you the women in Paul's day saw liberty in every word of that command, and so did the men, I'm sure, once they understood all that it meant. The call is to give ourselves sexually to each other freely and without reserve. Note the equality of rights. It is not the husband's rights and the wife's duties. There is mutual giving and receiving. Men, your wife deserves to be satisfied sexually. You are free within the covenant of marriage to do whatever would delight, whatever would please, whatever would satisfy. And women have the same liberty.

Coitus has larger purposes than procreation. Children are great, to be sure, but we must never confine sex to "baby making." Intimacy, self-disclosure, vulnerability, recreation—these and more all inform the sexual experience.

One of the great things about sex is the warmth, the love, the indefinable sense of knowing someone in the most intimate way possible. It is no accident that the Hebrew term for coitus is *yada'*, "to know." The sexual experience somehow ushers us into the subterranean chambers of each other's being.

No doubt the experience of self-disclosure and vulnerability that goes hand in hand with sexual intercourse contributes to this mysterious sense of knowing. There is something to the unashamed nakedness, the total giving of oneself that allows a couple to crash through the sound barrier of external niceties and into the inner circle of nearness. There is a sense in which the physical coupling is indicative of a deeper coupling—a uniting of heart, mind, soul, and spirit. It's wonderful, it's good, and even more, it's fun.

It is this aspect of fun, of recreation, that is, in many ways, the richest experience of all. Sex at its best, at its highest, at its holiest, is play. It is festivity; it is delight.

As C. S. Lewis said, "Banish play and laughter from the bed of love and you may let in a false goddess."[7]

We get to know each other in recreation in a way that is not possible when we are serious. Sex is an adventure; it is also a game. We delight in each other's bodies in a light, airy, happy way. We play together; we romp and frolic together. This is an essential element in our celebration of sex.

THE MEANING OF FIDELITY FOR THE CHURCH

We have tried to consider what the vow of fidelity might mean to single people and to married couples, but what about the corporate fellowship of believers? What does fidelity mean to the Church?

The first thing that we need to say to that question is that our understanding of what fidelity means must be drawn from the model we are given in God's covenant relationship with his people, and specifically Christ's fidelity to the Church. God's dogged faithfulness to his children in the Old Testament and Christ's tenacious love of his Church in the New Testament give us the content for the vow of fidelity. Our understanding of marriage must always be brought back to and judged by this paradigm. Paul puts it most graphically when he is dealing with the marriage union, "This is a great mystery, and I take it to mean Christ and the church." (Eph. 5:32).

When we understand marriage in light of God's covenant love for us, we are catapulted onto a new, positive level. Lewis Smedes writes, "The Christian concept of fidelity is based on the model offered to us by the marriage between God and his people. . . . If we use this model, we will avoid the sterile, passive caricature of fidelity that is mere absence of adultery. We will have a picture of someone who makes a solemn vow to enduring partnership and whose fidelity is measured in terms of creative love for his partner."[8] This model, however, can never remain theoretical. It must work its way into our practice. Let us turn, then, to the practical implications in the life of the Church.

The Church is first called to a ministry of prayer and spiritual direction. This is the business of the Church. Would to God that the Christian fellowship could provide an environment in which, for example, young couples could bring their questions about marriage and their leanings toward marriage to the fellowship for discernment, counsel, and blessing.

Not long ago I was part of a "meeting for clearness" for a young couple.* They were in love and everyone had encouraged them to get married, and yet they were not sure. They sought guidance from a group of spiritually discerning persons, and so we met together in our home for an afternoon. It was a precious time of laughing and praying and sharing with each other. During the course of the afternoon, the young woman, who was a "preacher's kid," shared that everything she had done all her life was, at least in part, because others wanted her to do it. She was always doing things to please her parents or to please the congregation, and she was afraid that she was entering into this marriage only because everyone else thought they were the "ideal couple." This, of course, was the key to the problem, and once it surfaced we were all able to look at it and deal with it. The final prayer of blessing that a woman minister in our group gave to the couple was deeply moving. She went over to them, laid her hands upon them, and prayed in such

---

* In simple terms a "meeting for clearness" is a gathering of spiritually discerning people to help an individual or couple discern the mind of God about a matter of concern to them. Corporately we are seeking "clearness" from the Lord. The most common matters that are brought to clearness meetings are marital decisions and vocational choices

tender and edifying words that I thought surely we were in heaven . . . and perhaps in a way we were. The two are now married and are vital members of our church fellowship. This was only one small event for a single couple, but this experience needs to be multiplied tens of thousands of times in churches everywhere.

There is so much more that we can do. We can all be glad for the good that has come from the Marriage Encounter movement that exists in many denominations, and we can only hope that it will increase. Here at the university, we have a program for engaged couples adapted from Marriage Encounter called Fit to Be Tied. As I write today, over fifteen couples are participating in this weekend experience and have just walked by my window on their way to the dining commons. Inwardly I pray for these marriages-to-be. What a wonderful ministry this program is! In this city we also have a program for people whose marriages are near shipwreck. We call it Recovery of Hope. It has been so well received that plans are now being made to establish it nationally. But these programs are only a drop in the bucket. The work is great and the laborers are few.

Church, do you get the idea? Stop wasting precious time and energy on committee meetings that discuss nothing. Stop carrying on business meetings that deal with everything except the business of the Church. Those marriages, those precious lives are the business agenda for the Church! Let us get on with it!

And then there are weddings. Even in our day of secularization, the Church still plays a prominent role in many weddings. Let us do something really significant with the opportunity. Let us have weddings that are genuine invitations to fidelity, to a lifetime call to marriage. Then the gathered fellowship can truly be "witnesses" to the rightness of marriages.

A few years back, I was at the wedding of a lovely

couple who had gone through a clearness meeting and who had asked the church to approve their intention for marriage which was done in a regularly called business session. Then at the wedding, rather than having the customary guest book, the couple had a large document that they asked all three hundred guests to sign as legal witnesses at the appropriate time in the ceremony. It was touching to walk to the front of the church and declare my conviction, both verbally and in writing, that I believed this marriage to be "in the Lord."

For the Church to "witness" and "bless" a marriage involves ongoing accountability for its success. We have dozens of useless committees; how about a useful one charged with encouraging the healthy growth and maturing of young marriages? Visiting homes, suggesting reading material, friendship counseling, and much more could make up the committee's agenda. And why not have another committee concerned with the health of established marriages?

We have a special service to begin marriages, why not a special service for the healing and blessing of existing marriages? Couples could come to the altar together; ministers could lay hands on them and offer prayers for the marriage to go from strength to strength.

C. S. Lewis has suggested that we need two kinds of marriages: one civil that is governed by the state and one Christian that is governed by the Church.[9] I agree. In this way the Church would be responsible for overseeing the health and success of Christian marriages. Marital problems, divorce, remarriage, and more would be issues for the community of faith to lovingly deal with. The believing fellowship would need to oversee the care of widows, widowers, divorcées, and the victims of desertion. In short, the care of Christian marriages would be the business of the Church.

THE SEXUALLY DISENFRANCHISED

We have been looking at what it means to be faithful before God with regard to our sexuality. In every case, we have taken for granted the fact that we are sexual beings. At no point did we need to convince ourselves of this fact. There are people, however, that have been shoved outside the world of sexualness. They have been thought of, by and large, as nonsexual beings. The vow of fidelity means a new awareness of and responsibility to the sexually disenfranchised.[10]

The physically disabled are considered nonsexual persons by many. The myth that the physically disabled are totally incapable of any sexual expression and therefore uninterested in sex only serves to isolate them all the more. However, studies have shown that even people with spinal cord injuries are often capable of *"achieving orgasm in spite of complete denervation of all pelvic structures."*[11]

How can we respond to the needs of the physically disabled? We can refuse to ignore their sexuality. We can recognize the wholesome value of fantasizing that can be so important to the sexual expression of the disabled. We can encourage couples to use a wide range of pleasuring techniques, all the way from stroking the face to oral-genital sex. One of the most valuable capabilities of the disabled is the ability to provide sexual pleasure to a spouse. Even if the individual is unable to experience orgasm, it is tremendously rewarding and stimulating to be able to give an orgasm to one's spouse.

Nor should we regard the seriously ill as nonsexual beings. The fact that death may be drawing near does not mean that all sexual interest and activity should or will disappear. "Indeed, the patient may often feel the desire for increased sexual activity with the spouse, as a way of clinging to life's vitalities and as a way of coping with death's anxieties."[12]

In spite of all the difficulties that the terminally ill face in carrying on a sexual life, it is often immensely rewarding. "Patients and their spouses report the deepening of their bonds and the clarifying of their real values. They report a more intense orientation to the possibilities of the present moment with each other, and the graceful appreciation of just being, not always doing."[13]

What can the Church do? Much. Let us train our pastors and chaplains to deal frankly and compassionately with this aspect of life rather than avoiding it. Let us encourage hospitals and other facilities to set aside rooms for conjugal visits. Maybe the Church could even volunteer to furnish rooms with large beds, soft lights, and comfortable furniture. Let us train ordinary folk in the pew in the healing art of touch—rubbing the back, combing the hair, holding the hand—intimate experiences all.

James Nelson tells the story of a colleague in the clergy that is a helpful illustration of the concern we should have for the need for intimacy of the seriously ill. " 'His mother was dying of cancer. Her body was clearly showing the ravages of the disease, and she was distressed by her altered appearance. On the one hand, she was resistant to the visits of those close to her because of her disfigurement. Yet, at the same time, her need for physical closeness and personal intimacy was great. Her son came to the hospital to visit, and as they talked, he rubbed her back to relieve some of the pain. After a time, sensing her need for even greater closeness, he lay down on the hospital bed beside her and held her closely in his arms. They talked for a long time that afternoon, sharing thoughts and feelings more deeply than ever before. Later that night she died.' It was, said my friend, clearly . . . an experience of physical closeness which deepened love's bonds and eased the pain of impending death."[14]

The aging is another group that we see as nonsexual. Our contemporary mania for identifying sex with youth and physical attractiveness only accentuates the problem. Yet the older members of our community continue to have sexual desires. The notion that the sex drive plummets rapidly to zero sometime after the age of sixty-five is simply false. Studies show that many people remain sexually active into their eighties and beyond.[15]

How can the Church respond? We can insist that nursing homes and retirement centers have facilities with beds large enough to allow married couples to sleep together. We can encourage widowed persons to remarry if they wish to rather than stay "faithful" to the dead spouse. We can work to change the Social Security laws so that remarriage for the elderly will not be an economic liability. We can give social permission for masturbation and allow for the needed privacy. We can encourage touching, holding, hugging.

Lastly, there is the mentally retarded. Often we think of these good people as nonsexual beings, but research indicates just the opposite. The overwhelming majority are keenly aware of their own sexuality, and most are very aware of their own genital needs and desires. Unfortunately, the institutional environment is usually not conducive to wholesome sexual development. Men and women are frequently segregated; there is seldom any privacy.

What can we do? We can insist that the mentally retarded receive as much sex education as is feasible. Studies show keen interest by the mentally retarded in learning about their sexuality. They are left out of so much of life; it is wrong to withhold sex education if we can possibly do otherwise.

The question of sterilization of the mentally retarded must be handled with great sensitivity. On the one hand, individual rights must be protected and, on the other hand, genetic mental retardation needs to be curbed. If the matter of unwanted pregnancy can be resolved, we can encourage the possibility of marriage. The mentally retarded have as great a capacity for love and relationship as you or I, perhaps greater. We should not deny them this opportunity. When marriage is undertaken, then allowance should be made for the couple to live together, even if it is within the institution.

FIDELITY IN PERSPECTIVE

We have sought to travel a long way. We have looked at the vow of fidelity for the single, for the married, and for the Church. We have considered a few ways we can respond to the sexually disenfranchised. Always remember, fidelity is not a static set of regulations; it is a vibrant, living adventure. It is not so much a way to suppress lust as a way to orient our lives toward a unifying goal. Fidelity is the sine qua non of unity and focus.

PART III

Power

10. Destructive Power

We live in a world possessed. And we know it.
—JOHAN HUIZINGA

If money hits us in the pocketbook, and sex hits us in the bedroom, power hits us in our relationships. Power profoundly impacts our interpersonal relationships, our social relationships, and our relationship with God. Nothing touches us more profoundly for good or for ill than power.

Power can destroy or create. The power that destroys demands ascendency; it demands total control. It destroys relationship; it destroys trust; it destroys dialogue; it destroys integrity. And this is true whether we look through the macrocosm of human history or the microcosm of our own personal histories.

What does the power that destroys look like? Think of Adam and Eve in the garden—given every pleasure, every delight, everything necessary for a good life. Yet they wanted more; they grasped and grabbed in a headlong rush to be like God, to know good and evil. *The sin of the garden was the sin of power.* They wanted to be more, to have more, to know more than is right. Not content to be creatures, they wanted to be gods.

That spirit festers within us, doesn't it? For us, it is never enough to enjoy good work. No, we must obtain supremacy; we must possess; we must hoard; we must conquer. The sin of power is the yearning to be more than we are created to be. We want to be gods.

Philosophy professor Arthur Roberts speaks of the little tin idols we make of ourselves in type and the colored mirror, television.¹ We chase our reflected image down broad highways and fling our metal birds at the planets. "Hallelujah to us!" we shout. But the sounds hurt our ears, and the sights burn our eyes, and the ashes fill our mouths, and the whole thing stinks to high heaven. And God, watching, weeps.

For Adam and Eve, the will to power meant a rupture in their relationship with God. The experience of communion and dialogue with God was broken. They hid from him. We, too, hide from God. The will to power ruptures our relationship with him. Our headstrong determination to do it our way makes God's voice distant and his word hard to hear.

What does the power that destroys look like? Think of King Saul and his insane envy of David. Saul was the king; he was supposed to wield the power. But power cannot command affection, and the people loved David. Saul was powerless to control the hearts of people, so he turned in rage against David. He would rather have murdered than allow power to slip through his fingers. How tragic to see the relationship between Saul and David destroyed because of Saul's lust for power. It even destroyed Saul's relationship with his own son Jonathan.

Power destroys relationships. Lifelong friends can turn into mortal enemies the moment the vice-presidency of the company is at stake. Climb, push, shove is the language of power. Nothing cuts us off from each other like power. Even ordinary human conversation is destroyed by it. Paul Tournier writes, "Power is the greatest obstacle in the way of dialogue. . . . We pay dearly for our power; we live the drama of the lost dialogue."² And we see this tragic drama everywhere: between husband and wife, between parent and child, between employer and employee. Power's ability to destroy human relationships is written across the face of humanity.

What does the power that destroys look like? Think of

the disciples arguing bitterly over who would be the greatest in the kingdom of God. These arguments must have been intense, because they are mentioned in all four Gospels. The end result of this constant bickering and jockeying for position was the undermining of harmony among the apostolic band. From that point on, they would have been suspicious of each other's motives.

Amazing isn't it, grown-up people deeply exercised over who is at the top of the heap! Of course, whenever we are deciding who is the greatest, we are also deciding who is the least. This is the problem for us, isn't it? To be the least means to be helpless. If we are at the "bottom rung" of a company, we are completely without authority, completely without power.

Whenever this argument came up among the disciples, Jesus would sit a child in the middle of the group and teach them about greatness. What was he doing? He was pointing to the ability of children to work and play without the need for supremacy. Have you ever watched little children in the backyard making mud pies? You see, they are simply content to make mud pies while the rest of the world goes on in its mad rush for "greatness." It reminds me of Tolkien's description of Aüle, one of the original eight guardians and governors of Middle Earth, "But the delight and pride of Aüle is in the deed of making, and in the thing made, and neither in possession nor in his own mastery; wherefore he gives and hoards not and is free from care, passing ever on to some new work."[3] You see, in the kingdom of God the issue of greatness is an issue that is beside the point. Others may fight and struggle over the question of who is the greatest, but for the disciple of Christ it is a virtue to ignore the question. Paul says, "There is great gain in godliness with contentment" (1 Tim. 6:6).

What does the power that destroys look like? Think of Simon Magnus and his desire to merchandise the Holy

Spirit (Acts 8:9-25). Simon was a magician in Samaria who evidently had considerable power, because the people said of him, "This man is that power of God which is called Great" (Acts 8:10). Simon, however, came under the influence of Philip's preaching and was converted to faith in Jesus Christ. Later Peter and John came to Samaria and laid hands on the people, and they received the Holy Spirit. When Simon saw the power that came through the laying on of hands, he "offered them money, saying, 'Give me also this power, that any one on whom I lay my hands may receive the Holy Spirit'" (Acts 8:18-19). Peter, of course, rebuked him for thinking he could merchandise the power of God, and we are given indication that Simon repented of his evil intent.

The sin of Simon Magnus was to try to use the power of God for his own ends. This is the sign of all false religion, but it is exactly this mentality that has come over so much of Christianity in our day. Cheryl Forbes writes, "The cassock of righteousness becomes the vestment of power."[4]

Power can be an extremely destructive thing in any context, but in the service of religion it is downright diabolical. Religious power can destroy in a way that no other power can. Power corrupts, and absolute power corrupts absolutely; and this is especially true in religion. Those who are a law unto themselves and at the same time take on a mantle of piety are particularly corruptible. When we are convinced that what we are doing is identical with the kingdom of God, anyone who opposes us *must* be wrong. When we are convinced that we always use our power to good ends, we believe we can never do wrong. But when this mentality possesses us, we are taking the power of God and using it to our own ends.

Those who are accountable to no one are especially susceptible to the corrupting influence of power. It was precisely this problem that caused Saint Benedict to establish the rule of stability. In the sixth century there were many wandering prophets and monks with no one to hold them accountable for what they said or did. But with the rule of stability they were drawn into communities in which mutual encouragement and discipline were possible. Today, most media preachers and itinerant evangelists suffer from exactly the same lack of accountability that the wandering prophets of the sixth century did. What is needed today is a modern Benedictine rule that would draw these powerful leaders into a disciplined and accountable fellowship.

What we must see is the wrongness of those who think they are always right. Jesus Christ alone is always right. The rest of us must recognize our own foibles and frailties and seek to learn from the correction of others. If we do not, power can take us down the path of the demonic.

PRIDE AND POWER

There is an intimate connection between pride and the destructive character of power. Samson was a man of immense power, power that was given by God. But pride filled his heart, and not only pride but arrogance as well. Before his enemies Samson boasts, "With the jawbone of an ass have I slain a thousand men" (Judg. 15:16). This unholy trinity of pride, arrogance, and power contributed to Samson's downfall.

Power is insidious when it is coupled with pride. Among the most dangerous people in our media-soaked culture are leaders who believe their own press releases. I remember once being honored at a large conference. I could only stay for twenty-four hours because of family commitments. The time was full of special luncheons and autograph parties and media interviews. By the end of the twenty-four hours, I told Carolynn, "We have to get out of here; I'm beginning to believe all these things people are saying about me." One can quickly lose all perspective. That is why those in positions of leadership must root themselves deeply in the experiences of ordinary life.

Of course, all of us suffer from vanity's lures, not just leaders. But leaders are especially susceptible today because of our infatuation with the media. Isn't it strange, for example, that we unquestionably assume that being on television is some kind of honor? Somehow we feel that television defines who the important people are. The idea is really silly, of course, but we hold to it nonetheless. In *Christ and the Media*, Malcolm Muggeridge suggests that if Jesus were going through the wilderness temptation today Satan would add a fourth temptation, namely, to appear on national television.

All of this makes pride one of the monumental problems of our day. Isn't it instructive that in a day when so many people struggle desperately for self-esteem we also have an abundance of people with over-inflated egos? When pride is mixed with power the result is genuinely volatile. Pride makes us think we are right, and power gives us the ability to cram our vision of rightness down everyone else's throat. The marriage between pride and power carries us to the brink of the demonic.

THE PRINCIPALITIES AND THE POWERS

The demonic is precisely where destructive power reaches its apex. The Bible speaks of very real cosmic spiritual powers that manifest themselves in the very real structures of our very real world. The apostle Paul's favorite term to describe this spiritual reality is "the principalities and powers," though he uses other terms as well—"authorities," "dominions," "thrones," "rulers," "the elemental spirits of the universe," "princes of this world," and still others. These "powers" account for the destructive bent of power that we see all around us. Indeed, it is only as we begin to understand what the Bible calls "the principalities and powers" that we can truly confront the power issue in our own lives.

We must not dismiss this teaching as the relic of a prescientific era. The Bible is dealing with a far more profound reality than forked-tailed demons in red pajamas or benign ghosts. The powers are not spooks floating around in the air preying on unwary individuals but spiritual realities that play a definite role in the affairs of human beings.

The powers are created realities. Paul tells us that in Christ "all things were created, in heaven and on earth, visible and invisible, whether thrones or dominions or principalities or authorities—all things were created through him and for him" (Col. 1:16). The powers were once related to the creative will of God; however, we no longer see them in this role. They are in revolt and rebellion against God their Creator. Our warfare, says Paul, is "against the principalities, against the powers, against the world rulers of this present darkness, against the spiritual hosts of wickedness in the heavenly places" (Eph. 6:12). Indeed, the Bible speaks of the powers as gods that seek to enslave and destroy (Gal. 4:8-10).

The powers are incarnational. They are the energizing forces behind human beings and social structures. When Paul tells us that the powers "crucified the Lord of glory," he is emphasizing that the crucifixion of Christ was far more than the work just of human personalities (1 Cor. 2:8). *

---

* First Corinthians 2:8 reads, "None of the rulers of this age understand this; for if they had, they would not have crucified the Lord of glory." "The rulers of this age" is a phrase that Paul uses to describe the powers. Almost all commentators agree that Paul here is not speaking of human beings but of superearthly realities. See Chapter 2 of *Christ and the Powers* by Hendrik Berkhof for more information (trans. John H. Yoder [Scottdale, Penn.: Herald Press, 1962]).

The powers, however, do not "possess" just individuals but organizations and whole structures of society. Institutions can and do often become nothing more than organized sin. There are fundamental spiritual realities that underlie all political, social, and economic systems. In back of brutal dictators and unjust policies and corrupt institutions are spiritual principalities and powers. Walter Wink writes, "the 'principalities and powers' are the inner and outer aspects of any given manifestation of power. As the inner aspect they are the spirituality of institutions, the 'within' of corporate structures and systems, the inner essence of outer organizations of power. As the outer aspect they are political systems, appointed officials, the 'chair' of an organization, laws—in short, all the tangible manifestations which power takes. Every Power tends to have a visible pole, an outer form—be it a church, a nation, or an economy—and an invisible pole, an inner spirit or driving force that animates, legitimates, and regulates its physical manifestation in the world."[5]

When the apostle Paul says that our warfare is not against flesh and blood but against the principalities and powers, he does not mean that flesh and blood are unimportant. Not at all! He means that the real focus of our battle should be the powers that stand in back of the person or institution.

Organizations and whole nations are often defined and controlled by particular concepts and ideologies. There is a prevailing mood or spirit that gives unity and direction to whole groups of people. These moods are not created in a vacuum, but are closely tied to very genuine spiritual realities. Hence, when we speak of "the spirit of a group" we are perhaps saying more than we know.

For example, when Ku Klux Klan members gather together, the collective hatred is something that is greater than the sum of its parts. When a certain critical flashpoint of prejudice and ruthlessness is reached, a "mob spirit" erupts that no single individual is able to control. Spiritual powers are involved in the creation of such realities.

This is a terribly difficult concept for us to comprehend in our modern society. We are accustomed to viewing institutions as sterile, neutral structures that have nothing to do with the spiritual life. There has been, however, one outstanding historical event that can help us develop a new appreciation for the biblical emphasis upon the powers. When Adolf Hitler took over Germany, the powers of state and race took on hideous new dimensions. In the Third Reich the very idea of *volk*—race—became captive to the egomania of Aryan supremacy. Those who have seen the crematories of Dachau and Auschwitz do not find it hard to believe in the demonic powers.

What does this mean to us on a practical level? Well, when we look at our own insane drive to make it to the top, we must confront the powers of pride and prestige that grip our hearts. When there is a school board decision that does a disservice to children, we must confront the powers of vested interest and self-seeking that stand behind that decision. We must seek out the "spirit" that energizes the unjust law or the unjust corporate structure and seek to defeat *it* in the power of Christ.

DISCERNING THE POWERS

Amazing as it may seem, it is the Church's awesome responsibility to discern these spiritual powers. Among the gifts that the Holy Spirit gives to the people of God is the discernment of spirits (1 Cor. 12:8-10). We are given the ability to recognize the powers for what they are and to understand their hostility to the way of Christ.

Discerning the powers is not as easy as we may think at first. For example, when Hitler began his rise to power in Germany, he campaigned on a 25-point platform that included a vigorous German nationalism, a pledge to improve educational opportunities, a concern for "raising the standard of health in the nation," and a belief in "positive Christianity."[6] Now, you and I can look back on the Third Reich and easily see its demonic perversion, but in the midst of that wrenching experience virtually the only Christians who had eyes to see the hellish powers behind the Third Reich were the Confessing Church.* Pastor Martin Niemöller saw; Reich Bishop Müller did not.

This ministry of discerning the powers, fraught as it is with frustrations and pitfalls, is given to you and to me. We are to discern what is truly happening today, understand where it could lead us, and give a value judgment upon it.

Saint Francis of Assisi saw the people of his day in the grip of the power of mammon, and he joyfully called them to a new way. Once a man named Silvester saw Francis and Bernard distributing money to the poor; he was "seized with greed" and said to Francis, "You did not pay me all you owe me for those stones you bought from me to repair the churches." Saint Francis just stood there "marveling at his greed" and finally reached both hands into the money bag and gave to Silvester all the money his hands could hold. He then said, "If you ask for more, I will give you still more." Silvester went home with the money, but he soon "reproached himself for his greed." For three nights straight he had a

---

* The "Confessing Church" (Bekennende Kirche) was composed of Christians in Germany who opposed the takeover of the Church by Hitler's ecclesiastical puppet, Reich Bishop Müller. They drafted the famous Barman Confession of May 1934 which categorically rejected the supremacy of the state over the Church and confessed the Lordship of Jesus Christ. Among their leaders were Karl Barth, Martin Niemöller, and Dietrich Bonhoeffer.

vision from God telling him that Saint Francis was the one who had the true wealth. In the end, Silvester was freed from the spirit of greed and was enabled to give generously to the poor; in time he became "so holy and filled with grace that he spoke with God as one friend to another."[7]

What happened? Saint Francis had discerned the spiritual power of greed that possessed Silvester, and he was able, in the power of God, to free him from it.

How desperately we need to be freed from greed today! It is a spiritual power that grips us. The whole ethos of our nation is possessed by it. It exists at every level of society. If Christians would take the initiative in bringing about a national exorcism of greed, we might be able to open our hearts and hands to a hungry world once again.

Nearly a hundred and fifty years before the Civil War, John Woolman saw dire consequences for our bondage to the powers of racism and oppression. "I saw a dark gloominess hanging over the Land," he wrote. If people were not willing to "break the yoke of oppression," he saw that "the Consequence will be grievous to posterity."[8] It is a genuine tragedy that we as a nation were unwilling to heed his prophetic discernment. As G. M. Trevelyan has said, "Close your ears to John Woolman one century, and you will get John Brown the next, with Grant to follow."[9]

How desperately we need to be free of the spiritual powers of racism and oppression! These demons of the spirit are on the rise today. We can all be glad for the advances made during the civil rights movement, but we are now seeing alarming reversals. Would to God that Christians could lead the way to a new day of justice and brotherhood. It will happen if we can discern the powers and seek their defeat in the strength of the Lamb.

NAMING THE POWERS

"Test the spirits," says John (1 John 4:1). This is a task fraught with pitfalls, but one we cannot avoid. How do the powers manifest themselves today?

Mammon is one of the powers. Paul Tournier notes that, "the GNP is the modern Golden Calf."[10] Our wealth is not neutral. It is not sterile or inanimate. It is alive with spiritual power; it seeks to possess us. In Part I we took a long look at how we can conquer mammon in the power of the Lamb and bring it back to its divine intent.

Sex is one of the powers. Sex in our day is not just a need, like cheerful surroundings or friendly conversation. It is a power energized by lust, sensuality, and uncontrolled carnality. For untold millions it is an all-consuming passion. We cannot hear the old cliché, "Keep her barefoot in the winter and pregnant in the summer," without recognizing the language of power. We cannot look at the crimes of incest and rape without realizing that these are crimes of power. Sex is power, real power. There is nothing neutral or passive about it. It is alive with spiritual energy seeking to make a bid for supremacy over the hearts of men and women. In Part II we dealt with ways we can defeat the carnality of sexuality and bring it back to its God-given function of enriching human relationships.

Religious legalism is one of the powers. Paul declares, "If with Christ you died to the elemental spirits of the universe, why do you live as if you still belonged to the world? Why do you submit to regulations, 'Do not handle, Do not taste, Do not touch' . . . according to human precepts and doctrines?" (Col. 2:20-22). These "elemental spirits" are religious and ethical rules. Paul's point is that behind the religious traditions and regulations are spiritual powers, powers that have claimed autonomy and have made obedience to them the highest good.

The tragedy here is that the very thing that is designed

to lead us to God does exactly the opposite. The divine function of moral law is to bring us into obedience, but when it becomes an end in itself the demonic perversion called legalism rears its ugly head. These rules and regulations become rival gods holding us captive and demanding our total allegiance.

Religious legalism is one of the heaviest burdens human beings ever have to bear. Jesus warns us of those who will "bind heavy burdens, hard to bear, and lay them on men's shoulders; but they themselves will not move them with their finger" (Matt. 23:4).

Technology is one of the powers. In the broad sense, technology standardizes procedures and behavior in order to produce efficiency. In fact, efficiency is the sacred law of technology. Of course, there is nothing wrong with efficiency and productivity—not until it becomes an ultimate value. "Technology tends more and more to become a new god," notes John Wilkinson.[11]

When efficiency becomes a new god, we have the supremacy of standardization over spontaneity. We all feel this, don't we? When we receive a telephone call from a computer we know that efficiency has won over spontaneity. When we fill out punch cards that ask for numbers rather than names, we know that standardization has won over individuality. We have become things and we sense deep inside that our personhood has been violated.

When we say, "If it is efficient it *must* be good," we have given ultimate significance to technology. For the Christian, other questions must counterbalance the question of efficiency: Will human beings be crushed in the process? Will it damage individual self-esteem? These and many other questions need to be considered as we seek to discern the spirituality of technology and to respond to it appropriately.

Narcissism is one of the powers. Narcissism is exces-

sive self-love, and it is the dominant mood of our age.
Pleasure seeking and self-satisfaction are at the top of the
priority list. Advertisers scream, "Grab all the gusto you
can get," and we sing, "I did it my way." The very idea
of sacrifice for the good of others seems ludicrous.

We must reject the narcissism of our age. We as believers know that the good life is not found in selfishness
but in self*less*ness. We who follow the crucified Christ
know that to lose ourselves is to find ourselves (Luke 9:
24–25).

Militarism is one of the powers. The divine purpose of
military power is to restrain chaos, but in our day militarism is doing precisely the opposite. Today the purpose is
not to prevent chaos but to promote it. Military strategists
plot, not how to make the world more stable, but how to
make it less stable. Terrorism and spy networks are the
order of the day.

In saying this, I am not criticizing any particular nation
or institution or group. In our day the creation of chaos
has become an all-pervasive mood of militarism. The final
end of this demonic perversion is the ultimate exercise of
power in destroying the world. Christians must call
militarism away from its evil bent.

Absolute skepticism is one of the powers. Absolute
skepticism is so pervasive a belief in university life today
that it must be considered a spiritual power hostile to an
honest search for truth. The task of the university is to
pursue truth—all truth—and yet in many cases precisely
the reverse is happening today. What was once a humble
position of genuine agnosticism has been turned into the
arrogance of absolute skepticism. Not knowing, not being
sure, becomes the final dogma that must never be violated.

C. S. Lewis, in his novel *That Hideous Strength*, depicts
the ultimate destructiveness of the university when it is
given over to deception and a desire to obscure the truth.

We must call the university back to its humble mission of truth seeking. The university should be the place par excellence where the big questions of purpose, meaning, and values are relentlessly pursued, and when answers are found they should be embraced and not denied.

Demonic spiritual powers have a pronounced impact upon the world in which we live. They stand behind, influence, and energize evil individuals and institutions. They manifest themselves in such things as mammon, sex, religious legalism, technology, narcissism, militarism, and absolute skepticism.

DEFEATING THE POWERS

We must never fool ourselves. The powers against which we wage the Lamb's war are very strong. Satan prowls about like a "roaring lion" seeking those whom he may devour (1 Pet. 5:8). This is no minor league game we are playing; we are in the major leagues, and the stakes are high. The principalities and powers do not just have power—they *are* power. They exist as power; power is how they manifest themselves. To dominate, to control, to devour, to imprison, is their very essence. How then do we defeat the demons without and the monsters within?

First, we must recognize that Christ has already defeated the powers. In his death and resurrection, Christ "disarmed the principalities and powers and made a public example of them, triumphing over them in him" (Col. 2:15). On the cross Christ could have summoned ten thousand angels to his aid, but instead he renounced the mechanisms of power in order to defeat the powers of the abyss. In the death and resurrection of Jesus Christ, the powers were defeated here in our time-space-energy-mass world.

Second, we defeat the powers by cultivating the gift of

discernment. Any serious engagement with the powers necessitates the "discerning of spirits" (1 Cor. 12:10, KJV). Until we have eyes to see the spiritual powers that energize a family, a corporate structure, or a government agency we do not fully understand it.

You may wonder how such a discerning spirit is obtained. It comes first by asking for it. "You do not have, because you do not ask," said James (James 4:2). We ask. We also listen: listen to God, listen to those around us, listen to what is occurring in our world. And we invite God to teach us what it all means. We also gather in groups of faithful believers to share insights and to listen together, for no single individual can know all of God's will. We do all this with a good deal of humor and humility: humor, because we must never take ourselves too seriously; humility, because we must take God's word through others with utmost seriousness.

Third, we defeat the powers by forthrightly facing the "demons" within. Right at the outset, we all need to see and to address the powers that nip at our own heels. Otherwise we will utilize the tactics of the very powers we oppose and, in the end, become as evil as they. We must look squarely into the face of our own greed and lust for power and see them for what they are. We must look at ourselves spiritually and discern ourselves spiritually.

The glory is that we do not do this alone. The blessed Holy Spirit comes alongside of us and comforts and encourages as he convicts and reproves. He leads us into the inner solitude of the heart where he can speak to us and teach us. Sometimes this will take the form of private retreat for prayer and reflection. More often it will be an inner retreat of the heart in the midst of life's many activities and demands. In this interior silence we hear the *Kol Yahweh*, the voice of the Lord. Hearing, we turn from our violence, our greed, our fear, our hate. Hearing, we turn to Christ's love and compassion and peace. We rejoice over every conquest of the Lamb, and as the Lamb conquers and wins our hearts, every victory feast has a place setting for our enemies.

Fourth, we defeat the powers by an inner renunciation of all things. In a posture of total renunciation, we have nothing to lose; the powers have no control over us. Suppose the powers take our goods and possessions—no matter, our possessions are only on loan from God; protecting them is more his business than it is ours. Suppose the powers seek to destroy our influence by defaming our reputation—no matter, our reputation is not ours to protect, and we could not do it even if we wanted to. Suppose the powers throw at us the fear of death itself—no matter, we belong to One who can lead us through death's dark pathway into greater life. So, you see, we simply have nothing to lose. We are positionless and possessionless, and this complete and total vulnerability is our greatest strength. You cannot take something from someone who has nothing.

Fifth, we defeat the powers by rejecting the weapons of power of this world. We stop trying to manage and control others. We refuse to dominate or intimidate. As Walter Wink has written, "The direct use of power against a Power will inevitably be to the advantage of The Powers That Be."[12]

The only way we can battle the principalities and powers is in the life and power of the Holy Spirit. Now, in saying this I am not trying to catapult this entire issue into the realm of the pietistic or the theoretical. Quite the contrary. The Holy Spirit wants to be an active agent in our lives in the most practical and socially concrete way.

If we attack the form of power alone without defeating the angel or spirit that energizes that form, we have accomplished nothing. For example, most revolutions in the world have struggled to throw out one corrupt and self-serving government only to have another corrupt and self-serving government take its place. The failure is to understand that the real battle has more to do with the powers of greed, vested interest, and egomania than with actual persons and structures of government. We must focus our attention on both the institution *and* the spirituality of the institution.

Sixth, we defeat the powers by using the weapons of Ephesians 6. To reject the weapons of this world does not leave us defenseless. Far from it! Who needs guns and tanks and MX missiles when we are given the far greater weapons of truth, righteousness, peace, faith, salvation, the word of God, and prayer (Eph. 6:10-18)! These weapons are more powerful than we can possibly imagine. Paul insists that "the weapons of our warfare are not worldly but have divine power to destroy strongholds" (2 Cor. 10:4).

Often we have rendered these spiritual weapons harmless by ignoring the social context of the Ephesians passage. We have turned them into pietistic weapons that have nothing to do with the world of mammon or militarism. We talk glibly of Roman shields and helmets and never once guess that we are called to arm ourselves for a real battle against the spirituality of institutions and cultures and all forms of demonic incarnation.

Another way we have sought to sterilize these weapons is by teaching that they are all "defensive." This is simply not the case. The Roman military was the most powerful and ruthless killing machine of that day. The equipment Paul describes was not solely for standing one's ground, but for advancing against the enemy. No doubt Paul had in mind the "Roman wedge," which was an effective V-shaped formation that made full use of a specially designed, elongated shield with which a soldier covered two-thirds of his own body and one-third of his comrade to the left. This ingenious arrangement forced soldiers to work together for mutual protection and attack. It was "the most efficient and terrifying military formation known up to that time and for some thousand years after."[13]

Paul's military metaphor is a wonderful picture of the company of the committed working in concert, advancing against the powers, conquering in Christ's name. The gates of hell cannot stand against such a unified and determined offensive. James Nayler writes, "He [Christ] puts spiritual weapons into their hearts and hands. . . . to make war with his enemies, conquering and to conquer, not as the prince of this world . . . with whips and prison, tortures and torments on the bodies of creatures, to kill and destroy men's lives . . . but with the word of truth . . . returning love for hatred, wrestling with God against the enmity, with prayers and tears night and day, with fasting, mourning and lamentation, in patience, in faithfulness, in truth, in love unfeigned, in long suffering, and in all the fruits of the spirit, that if by any means he may overcome evil with good."[14]

A PERSONAL REFLECTION

C. S. Lewis notes that "there are two equal and opposite errors into which our race can fall about the devils. One is to disbelieve in their existence. The other is to believe and to feel an excessive and unhealthy interest in them. They themselves are equally pleased by both errors and hail a materialist or a magician with the same delight."[15] If we err today it is usually in the direction of the materialist, for that is the dominant mood of our age. Normally I am hesitant to interject personal experiences but in this case I think it might be helpful.

Although I had finished writing this book, I did not feel satisfied with these last chapters on power. So I sent the first nine chapters to my editor, explaining that I had decided to rewrite the final four. By Wednesday of the first week of rewriting I began to sense a heaviness and darkness come over me. I am sure it was partly due to emotional and physical weariness with the task, for I had been writing for nine months with hardly a break and had done considerable research before that. (I had, however, been very careful to discipline myself to obtain adequate sleep and exercise.)

By Friday the darkness was nearly overwhelming. I felt as though I never wanted to write again, speak again or teach again. I would look over a chapter and want to throw it away. I tried to think of some way to cancel the entire project. Even now, I cannot fully explain what I was feeling. To use the words of George Fox, I was nearly overcome by an "ocean of darkness."[16]

Anyone who has studied psychology will know that what I am describing shows telltale signs of the beginning stages of exhaustion. That was certainly a factor in my experience, but it did not seem to account for everything I felt. There seemed to be more to it, some deeper greater foreboding.

On Saturday I went to my office to write, but with no hope of producing anything worth reading. During a period of meditation and prayer, I thought of the time Martin Luther threw his ink bottle at the devil. Instinctively I grabbed my pen and threw it against the wall, breaking it. I said to myself, "Well, if the devil is here I probably missed him!" I tried to arm myself with the weapons of Ephesians 6, but it seemed to do little good.

In the late morning a group of five friends came to pray for me. We talked only briefly, and then they prayed quietly. Though I cooperated with their efforts, I had absolutely no expectation that it would do any good. I felt nothing at all.

After they left, however, the heaviness began to lift just a bit. As the day went on, things got brighter and brighter, until by evening the darkness was completely gone. I was able then to finish my task without further oppression.

A few days later one member of the group that had come Saturday morning told me that during the prayer she had seen the entire room being filled with the light of Christ and the evil powers being thrust outside. I did not see anything, but I do not doubt her word, for she is a spiritually alert person and not in the least given to mystic fantasy. I believe her also because the ocean of darkness was indeed overcome by the ocean of light and life.

All of this may sound strange to you, but it did happen, and perhaps it can stand as a witness that the principalities and powers are real and do indeed wage war against us. It can also witness to the importance of having others who can help us as we do battle against the powers in this dark, evil age.

The powers are strong, but Christ is stronger still. The defeat of the powers is sure. We live in that life that overcomes the world, and we should expect to see the overthrow of the kingdom of darkness and the inauguration of the Lamb's rule of righteousness wherever we go.

11. Creative Power

The only cure for the love of power is the power of love.
—SHERRI McADAM

There is a power that destroys. There is also a power that creates. The power that creates gives life and joy and peace. It is freedom and not bondage, life and not death, transformation and not coercion. The power that creates restores relationship and gives the gift of wholeness to all. The power that creates is spiritual power, the power that proceeds from God.

What does the power that creates look like? Think of Joseph sold into slavery, thrown into prison without hope but later rising to a position of great power and influence in the mightiest nation of the time. What a pilgrimage! In this position Joseph was able to combine spiritual discernment with political clout to avert a disastrous famine. Then the fateful day arrived when his brothers—the very ones who had sold him into slavery—came seeking famine relief. Joseph was faced with the great test of power. It would have been a perfect opportunity for revenge, but instead he chose to use his power for reconciliation. Scripture tells us that Joseph was overcome with emotion and compassion for his brothers. Joseph "could not control himself" and "wept aloud," and finally "he fell upon his brother Benjamin's neck and wept; and Benjamin wept upon his neck. And he kissed all his brothers and wept upon them" (Gen. 45:1-15). This is a beautiful story of relationships restored by the exercise of creative power.

The power that creates is the power that restores relationships. William Wilburforce was a Christian politician who used the power of his position to help abolish the slave trade in the British Empire. The good of his prolonged efforts is beyond calculation. Families throughout Africa remained together because the gruesome British slave trade had been stopped. Talk about preserving relationships! And this is a story that could be repeated many times over as faithful believers have sought to apply God-given power creatively in the arena of politics and business.

The use of power to restore relationships is also a part of our personal, everyday world. The mother who rights a wrong between children is using her authority to restore broken relationships. The school principal who changes soul-destroying rules in the school system is breathing life into the hearts of students. The pastor who helps feuding committee members settle their differences is using power for healing in the community of faith. The company president who corrects the cost overruns of the project manager is using power to restore integrity and wholeness to the world of business. All of us in daily life encounter thousands of opportunities to enlist power in the service of reconciliation.

What does the power that creates look like? Think of Moses, who understood as few did the might and power of Egypt and who was forced to flee that power. In the desert he came to experience a new kind of power, the power of Yahweh. By the time Moses returned to face down the power of Egypt, he was a different person. Gone was the old arrogance; in its place was a new combination of meekness and confidence. The strong imperative "Let my people go" was backed up by the mighty acts of God, which brought even mighty Pharaoh to his knees. The result was the most dramatic release of captives ever known in human history.

Creative power sets people free. When Martin Luther

King, Jr., stood firm against America's racism, millions were set free. When teachers unlock the joy of discovery in the minds of students, they are using the power of their position to liberate. When an older brother uses his superior status to build the self-esteem of younger siblings, he is using power to set them free. When the old destructive habit patterns of depression or fear are transformed by the power of God, the result is liberation.

What does the power that creates look like? Think of Jeremiah, who remained true to the word of God in the most discouraging of circumstances. We call him the weeping prophet and for good reason. In a day when the religious leaders were catering their message to fit the prevailing political winds, Jeremiah spoke the *Dabar Yahweh*, the word of the Lord. That word was a discouraging one at best, a word of defeat and not of victory. And the people rejected Jeremiah's word of warning and even persecuted him. At one point he was thrown down a cistern and left to die. We are told that "Jeremiah sank in the mire" (Jer. 38:6). In many ways this simple statement is a good description of Jeremiah's entire ministry. He had to watch his beloved country overthrown and ravaged and his own people deported as spoils of war.

But it was the teaching of Jeremiah—the very teaching that the people had rejected—that enabled Judah to hold onto faith in Yahweh throughout the long years of exile. You see, the people had elevated their belief in the invincibility of Zion into a cardinal doctrine of their faith. And when Zion was destroyed, their whole belief system came crashing down. Hadn't God promised them Jerusalem would not fall? Where was God when the Babylonian hoards ravaged their land?

But Jeremiah had insisted over and over that Zion's invincibility was predicated upon obedience to the Mosaic Covenant, and because they had disobeyed the covenant, Zion would fall. God had not failed them by allowing

Jerusalem to fall; they had failed God by disobeying his covenant. Finally, Jeremiah spoke the words of hope and restoration and pointed to a new covenant, a covenant written not on tablets of stone but on the fleshy tablets of their hearts. "But this is the covenant which I will make with the house of Israel after those days, says the Lord: I will put my law within them, and I will write it upon their hearts, and I will be their God, and they shall be my people" (Jer. 31:33). It was Jeremiah's tenacity to the truth of Yahweh that enabled the people of Judah to keep faith in God when all the confident words of the false prophets were revealed as spurious.

Jeremiah reminds us that spiritual power sometimes looks like weakness. Faithfulness is more important than success, and the power to remain faithful is a great treasure indeed. Perhaps Jeremiah's word to his servant Baruch is good counsel for us today, "And do you seek great things for yourself? Seek them not" (Jer. 45:5).

Dietrich Bonhoeffer knew the power of God that looks like weakness to the world. "When Christ calls a man," he said, "he bids him come and die."[1] Bonhoeffer knew what it meant to die; he died to self, he died to all his hopes and dreams, and he died at the hands of Hilter's SS Black Guards. But as the Scripture reminds us, a grain of wheat that falls to the ground and dies bears much fruit (John 12:24). The fruit of Bonhoeffer's life and death is beyond calculation. We are all in his debt. As G. Leibholz has said, "Bonhoeffer's life and death has given us great hope for the future. . . . The victory which he has won was a victory for us all, a conquest never to be undone, of love, light and liberty."[2]

What does the power that creates look like? Think of the early church gathered at the Jerusalem Council (Acts 15). They had gathered to answer a momentous question: Can Gentiles have genuine faith in Christ without conformity to Jewish religious culture? It was an issue that could have easily split the Christian fellowship right down the middle. Yet as they gathered, as they talked, as they listened, the power of God broke through in a Spirit-led unity of heart and mind. Miraculously they saw that Gentiles could live faithfully before God within the context of their own culture and that Jews could do likewise. So the cultural captivity of the Church was broken, and believers everywhere could receive one another without needing to proselytize for their own culture. They experienced the power of unity in the Holy Spirit.

The power that creates produces unity. When John Woolman stood before the annual conference of the Quakers in 1758 and delivered his moving plea against slavery, the entire body, without spoken dissent, agreed to remove slavery from its midst. This unity of heart and mind is not easy to come by, but it is worth the effort. If we would learn to listen to the Lord together in our homes, in our churches, and in our businesses, we would see more of this unity of the Spirit. The family is the best place to begin. Father and mother can do much by leading the way in these matters.

What does the power that creates look like? Think of Jesus and his ministry of teaching and healing. Here we find the perfect display of perfect power. Everywhere he went, the powers of darkness were defeated, people were healed, relationships were restored. People came alive to God and alive to each other through the life-giving ministry of Jesus.

In the crucifixion the power that creates reached its apex. At the cross Satan sought to use all the power at his disposal to destroy Christ, but God turned it into the ultimate act of creative power. The penalty for sin was paid; the justice of God was satisfied. Through the cross of Christ, you and I can receive forgiveness and know the restoring of our relationship to God. Christ died for our sins, and in that death we see the power that creates.

Our response to this supreme act of power is gratitude. It is "love divine, all loves excelling." We can never hope or want to duplicate this act of power. We simply thank God for what he has done. Real forgiveness brings doxology. To know that God truly forgives all our sins and welcomes us into his presence is "joy unspeakable and full of glory." Doxology itself is power. As we live thankfully for God's great gift, others are drawn to know this joy of the Lord that overcomes all things.

THE MARKS OF SPIRITUAL POWER

The power that creates is spiritual power, and it is in stark contrast to human power. The apostle Paul spoke of the "flesh," and by it he meant human-initiated activity without the aid of divine grace. People can do many things in the power of the flesh, but they cannot do the work of the Spirit of God. The power of the flesh relies upon such things as proper pedigree, positions of status, and connections among those in the power structure. But Paul, you see, had given up on the flesh. He said that he counted those things as "dung," for his sights were set on a greater power, "that I may know him and the power of his resurrection, and may share his sufferings, becoming like him in his death, that if possible I may attain the resurrection from the dead" (Phil. 3:10–11).

Now, when we see people desperately scrambling for the "dung"— human power—we can be sure that they know precious little of the "power of his resurrection." What, then, are the marks of this power that proceeds from God?

Love is the first mark of spiritual power. Love demands that power be used for the good of others. Notice Jesus' use of power —the healing of the blind, the sick, the maimed, the dumb, the leper, and many others. Luke, the physician, observes that "all the crowd sought to touch him, for power came forth from him and healed them all" (Luke 6:19). Notice in each case the concern for the good of others, the motivation of love. In Christ, power is used to destroy the evil so that love can redeem the good.

Power for the purpose of advancing reputations or inflating egos is not power motivated by love. When God used Paul and Barnabas to heal a cripple at Lystra, the astonished people tried to turn them into Greek gods, but they tore their clothes and shouted out, "We also are men, of like nature with you" (Acts 14:15). Many of us might not find the idea of deity status so reprehensible. Think of the power over people we would have, and, after all, we would use the power to such good ends! But power that is used to advance reputations destroys the user, because with it we aspire to be gods.

This leads us to the second mark of spiritual power, humility. Humility is power under control. Nothing is more dangerous than power in the service of arrogance. Power under the discipline of humility is teachable. Apollos was a powerful preacher, but he was also willing to learn from others (Acts 18:24-26). In the course of his powerful ministry, Peter made some serious mistakes, but when confronted with his errors he had the humility to change (e.g., Acts 10:1-35; Gal. 2:11-21).

Believe me, this is no small matter. Many have been destroyed in their walk with God simply because their exercise of power was not controlled by humility. Power without humility is anything but a blessing.

James Nayler was one of the greatest of the early Quaker preachers. But he got carried away by his exercise of power, and in 1656 some of his wilder followers persuaded him to re-enact at Bristol Jesus' Palm Sunday ride into Jerusalem. This act proved to be his undoing. He was tried and convicted of blasphemy. The story does have a happy ending, for in time Nayler repented of his presumption, but he had lost his effectiveness in the service of Christ. Power destroys when it is not coupled with the spirit of humility.

To really know the power of God is to be keenly aware that we have done nothing more than to receive a gift. Gratitude, not pride, is our only appropriate response. The power is not ours, though we are given the freedom to use it. But when we truly walk with God, our only desire is to use power in the service of Christ and his kingdom.

This leads into the third mark of spiritual power, which is self-limitation. The power that creates refrains from doing some things—even good things—out of respect for the individual. Have you ever noticed the number of times Jesus refused to use power? He refused to dazzle people by jumping off the pinnacle of the temple (Matt. 4:5). He rejected the temptation to make more "wonder bread" to validate his ministry (John 6:26). He refused to do many wonderful works in his own hometown because of the unbelief of the people (Luke 4:16-27). He said no to the Pharisees' demand that he give a sign to prove he was the Messiah (Matt. 12:38). At his arrest, Jesus reminded Peter that he could have summoned a whole army of angels to his rescue, but he did not (Matt. 26:53).

The power that comes from the Holy Spirit is not to be used lightly. Paul said, "Lay hands suddenly on no man" (1 Tim. 5:22, KJV). We do people a disservice if we bring them into the power of God before they are ready. Those who live and move in God know that there is a time to withhold the hand of power just as there is a time to use it.

Joy is the fourth mark of spiritual power. This is no grim-faced, dour effort! Far from it! To see the kingdom of Christ break into the midst of darkness and depression is a wonderful thing. M. Scott Peck writes, "The experience of spiritual power is basically a joyful one."[3]

When the lame man was healed, he went "walking

and leaping and praising God" (Acts 3:8). That is a good description of our spontaneous reaction to the work of God. I once prayed with a veteran missionary over some deep inner hurts that stemmed from the tragic death of her son. As we prayed there was a very special sense of God's presence and then the clear release of the powers of fear and guilt. The Presence was so real, the release so definite, that we were both filled with a sense of wonder and awe. The time that has passed since those first prayer sessions has only validated what we experienced then. Months later, she wrote, "I have such peace. Rich, beautiful, holy joy lives inside me and just bubbles out. Finally, I know what Jesus meant when he said there would be rivers of living water flowing in us and through us. This is something I have looked for all my life."

I hope you understand that I am referring to something more profound than the bubbly "joy" of the superficial. The rich inner joy of spiritual power knows sorrow and is acquainted with grief. Joy and anguish often have a symbiotic relationship.

Vulnerability is the fifth mark of spiritual power. The power that comes from above is not filled with bravado and bombast. It lacks the symbols of human authority; indeed, its symbols are a manger and a cross. It is power that is not recognized as power. It is a self-chosen position of meekness that to human eyes looks powerless. It is the power of the "wounded healer," to use the phrase of Henri Nouwen.

The power from above leads from weakness. It is in contradiction to the society of the strong and the capable. Once when the apostle Paul was struggling with his own vulnerability the word of God came to him, saying, "My power is made perfect in weakness," and so he saw that "when I am weak, then I am strong" (2 Cor. 12:9-10).

What we often call the parable of the prodigal son might be more aptly called "the parable of the powerless almighty father."[4] In the father we see the power that does not dominate, the power that patiently waits. The parable is about God, of course: it is also a parable that was lived out in the life of Jesus. Look at him working patiently with stubborn, rebellious disciples. Look at him at his trial, speaking not a word. Look at him hanging on a wooden throne in total helplessness. These, I submit to you, are acts of spiritual power of the highest order.

In prison, Alexander Solzhenitsyn discovered that, whenever he tried to maintain a measure of power over his own life by acquiring food or clothing, he was at the mercy of his captors. But when he accepted and even embraced his own vulnerability, his jailers had no power over him. In a sense, he had become the powerful, they the powerless.[5]

We who understand the power of defenselessness may well have a genuine advantage. As our world becomes more complicated, the feeling of being powerless has become the order of the day. People we do not even know make decisions that affect us profoundly; we are not in control, and we know it. But the normal reactions of anger and resignation do not need to be ours, because we know what Jürgen Moltmann calls "the power of the powerless."[6]

The sixth mark of spiritual power is submission. Jesus knew what it meant to submit to the ways of God: "The Son can do nothing of his own accord, but only what he sees the Father doing; for whatever he does, that the Son does likewise" (John 5:19). As we learn to experience on a personal level this same kind of intimate cooperation with the Father, we will enter more deeply into the meaning of true power.

There is a power that comes through spiritual gifts, and there is a power that comes through spiritual positioning. The two work in unison. Submission gives us spiritual positioning. We are positioned under the leadership of Christ and under the authority of others. We find others in the Christian fellowship who can further us in the things of God. We submit to Scripture to learn more perfectly the ways of God with human beings. We submit to the Holy Spirit to learn the meaning of obedience. We submit to the life of faith in order to understand the difference between human power and divine power.

"Be subject to one another out of reverence for Christ," said Paul (Eph. 5:21). Paul himself was in submission to the church council at Jerusalem (Acts 15). Peter and Barnabas came under submission to Paul's correction when they failed to extend the right hand of fellowship to the Gentiles (Gal. 2:11-21). Apollos submitted to Aquila and Priscilla when it was clear that they knew more than he in the things of Christ (Acts 18:24-26).

Submission is power because it places us in a position in which we can receive from others. We are impoverished people indeed if our world is narrowed down to ourselves. But when, with humility of heart, we submit to others, vast new resources are opened to us. When we submit to others, we have access to their wisdom, their counsel, their rebuke, their encouragement.

Freedom is the final mark of spiritual power. People were set free when Jesus and the apostles exercised power. The lame could walk; the blind could see; the guilty knew forgiveness; and most wonderful of all, the demon-possessed were released. The powers of this dark evil age were defeated, and the captives were set free.

There is more, however, to this matter of freedom. Notice how Jesus worked with people. "He will not break a bruised reed or quench a smoldering wick," prophesied Isaiah (Matt. 12:20). And it was true. Jesus never ran roughshod over the weak. He never snuffed out even the smallest flicker of hope. He never used his power to exploit or to control others. It would have been easy for him to do otherwise. The poor who heard him so gladly would have done anything for him because they were so grateful just to have someone pay attention to them. But Jesus refused to exploit the power he had over them. No, he freed them to be themselves, fully and uniquely.

I once experienced this power that frees in an especially vivid way. I had just returned from a conference where I had made some rather significant decisions, and I was telling a friend who was a spiritual mentor about the experience. At one point I exclaimed, "Oh, by the way, I made one decision that I know you have been wanting me to make for a long time . . ." My friend interrupted, "Wait just a minute! Let's be clear about one thing. My business, my only business, is to bring the truth of God as I see it, and then to simply love you regardless of what you do or don't do. It is not my business to straighten you out or to get you to do the right thing." After our visit I thought about the significance of this simple statement. His care and compassion had always been evident, but in those words I discovered a new dimension of freedom—a freedom that allowed intimate friendship without a slavish need to please on either side. His power in my life is real, but it is a power that frees, not binds. Human power is power *over* someone, divine power has no such need to control — "*sine vi humana sed verbo*, 'without human power, simply by the word.' "[7]

POWER IN THE MARKETPLACE

This life-giving spiritual power is of value to us only as it is fleshed out in ordinary life. It will never do to speak piously of love, joy, and humility without rooting those realities in home, office, and school. What does spiritual power look like in the marketplace of life?

In the individual, power is to be used to promote self-control, not self-indulgence. Self-control is at home with both self-esteem and self-denial. Robert Schuller calls self-esteem *"the human hunger for the divine dignity that God intended to be our emotional birthright as children created in His image."*[8] Self-denial is the way this human hunger for self-esteem is satisfied, and self-control embraces them both.

Discipline is the language of self-control. The disciplined person is the person who can do what needs to be done when it needs to be done. The disciplined person is the person who can live appropriately in life. Such a person can laugh when laughter is appropriate, weep when weeping is appropriate, work when working is appropriate, play when playing is appropriate, pray when praying is appropriate, speak when speaking is appropriate, and be silent when silence is appropriate. Jean-Pierre de Caussade beautifully describes the life of self-control, "The soul, light as a feather, fluid as water, innocent as a child, responds to every movement of grace like a floating balloon."[9]

We experience control over self-indulgence by the power of God. Saint Francis called the human body "Brother Ass," because we are supposed to ride the ass rather than the ass riding us. It is self-control that gives us authority over "Brother Ass." From self-control comes freedom, for we are becoming what we were created to be.

In the home, power is to be used to nurture confidence, not subservience. How crucial it is for parents to use the authority they have over their children to build them up rather than tear them down, to encourage them rather than discourage them. A very wise parent once said to me, "Every 'No, no' must be matched by ten 'Atta boys.'" Criticism and correction is certainly necessary, but it must never be allowed to become destructive. As James Dobson says, we are "to shape the will of the child ... *but to do so without breaking his spirit."*[10] The use of power in the home can be a blessing if it is surrounded by a spirit of caring.

In the marriage, power is to be used to enhance communication, not isolation. Husbands and wives have power over each other, and they know it. All of us have certain things within us that will trigger utterly irrational reactions. When our spouse even comes near one of these issues, it is as though he or she has tripped a high-voltage lever. Knowledge is power, and in the intimacy of marriage we learn in explicit detail the nature of each other's "high-voltage levers." A particular topic or phrase, a certain way of acting, a particular tone of voice, even something as simple as the lift of an eyebrow or the shrug of a shoulder, can trigger these levers and start World War III.

These levers are real dynamite. Many times they have to do with old hurts and wounds in the marriage, and they have the power to block all genuine love and communication. But in the power of God we learn to lovingly avoid things that can be destructive to each other. We can also ask God to rewire our internal circuitry in such a way that these old hurts, these old wounds, are desensitized and no longer control us.

Our intimate knowledge of each other also means that we know what will enhance the relationship and encourage communication. We make use of this knowledge to open wide the channels of love and compassion.

In the Church, power is to be used to inspire faith, not conformity. Bishops, pastors, elders, deacons, and others have real power over people and should use it for life, not death. In matters that are essential to our spiritual growth, we want to do all we can to rouse people to action. But we must frankly admit that many things in our church life have little to do with righteousness, peace, and joy in the Holy Spirit. We do not need to proselytize people for our culture where it is not *necessary* as an expression of love of God and neighbor. In such matters we give people freedom in the gospel to be themselves without cultural conformity.

I remember so well "my pastor." I was young in both years and faith. I was also shy, and to compensate I would often show off and act boisterous. My pastor, however, bore patiently with me through those years of growing. He never tried to make me conform to the religious culture in the trivial matters of dress or speech. He gave me plenty of opportunity to struggle with theological issues, while at the same time setting forth clearly the fundamental tenets of the faith. I was inspired toward faith without conformity, a legacy for which I will always be grateful.

In the school, power is to be used to cultivate growth, not inferiority. Let us not kid ourselves; teachers and students are in a power relationship, but it can be a power to lift, not to destroy, if they understand their purpose. When teachers use their authority to stimulate children to learn, to think, to go on an adventure of discovery, they are engaging in a life-giving ministry. But it is very easy for a teacher to push too hard and to criticize too severely; when this happens, the child feels worthless. Teachers need to prod without demeaning, encourage excellence without depreciating those who fall short.

I vividly remember a teacher who prodded me to excellence without demeaning my shortcomings. He was a philosophy professor, and although I cannot remember all he taught me about Plato and Kierkegaard, I will never forget his love of words. He handled words in a way that was new for me: as a treasure to be cherished rather than propaganda to be maneuvered. He had a special regard for the mystery and power of words. In fact, words seemed to usher him into another world, a world in which I was a foreigner. I was very clumsy with words, so his skill with language frightened me as much as it intrigued me. He never depreciated me for my clumsiness but always urged me to try again. And I did try again, until I became at home in this world of words—a world in which zeal and insight meet in friendship, a world in which truth and beauty kiss each other. He was a teacher who saw past my feelings of inferiority and encouraged me to grow.

On the job, power is to be used to facilitate competence, not promote feelings of inadequacy. The business world is one place in which a Christian witness to creative power is desperately needed. Subordinates often feel helpless and manipulated, but it does not need to be this way. One thing all of us want to do is a good job. We want to know that we have made a genuine contribution, and we want to be competent in our area of service. Employers have the power to help realize this deep desire by providing opportunities for advanced training, by carefully delegating increased responsibility, and by helping employees realize their full potential. In fact, one definition of management is *"meeting the needs of people as they work at accomplishing their jobs."*[11]

The employee also has power, the power of encouragement. It may be hard for us to believe, but it is lonely at the top. Executives find that genuine friendships are hard to come by, because people fear their power. And those who do not fear it often are hoping to use it.

Employees who follow the way of Christ will reach out to their employers. They discern the hurt and loneliness of those who are over them. They give their friendship with no strings attached. They pray for their superiors and encourage them in every way possible. This, too, is a ministry of power.

THE POWER TO LIBERATE

We all exercise power over others. We are all affected by the power others exercise over us. We can choose the destructive power that is used to dominate and manipulate, or we can choose the creative power that is used to lead and liberate. It is only through the grace of God that we are able to take something as dangerous as power and make it creative and life-giving.

12. The Ministry of Power

In the mighty power of God go on!
—GEORGE FOX

Power touches us all. We cannot get away from it even if we wanted to. All human relationships involve the use of power. Therefore, rather than seek to run from it or to deny that we use it, we would do well to discover the Christian meaning of power and learn how to use it for the good of others. All who follow Christ are called to the "ministry of power."

POWER IN THE MINISTRY OF JESUS

Nothing is more clear than Jesus' consistent use of power to overthrow the kingdom of darkness and confirm his message that the kingdom of God has arrived. The Gospels are redundant with Jesus' ministry of casting out demons, healing the sick, and taking control over nature. Such demonstrations of kingdom power were not lost on the crowds: "When the multitudes saw it, they marvelled, and glorified God, which had given such power unto men" (Matt. 9:8, KJV).

Jesus' ministry was marked with authority. Spiritual power and spiritual authority are inseparable. In his Gospel, Mark tells of Jesus' healing of a demon-possessed person, adding that the people "were all amazed, so that they questioned among themselves, saying, 'What is this? A new teaching! With authority he commands even the unclean spirits, and they obey him'" (Mark 1:27). Jesus was not giving a new teaching; he was demonstrating a new power. He not only proclaimed the presence of the kingdom of God, he demonstrated its presence with power.

Now if Jesus had been the only one who exercised the ministry of power, we might be able to dismiss it as the privileged domain of the Messiah, but he delegated this same ministry to others. "And he called the twelve together and gave them power and authority over all demons and to cure diseases, and he sent them out to preach the kingdom of God and to heal" (Luke 9:1-2). That is precisely what they did, "And they departed and went through the villages, preaching the gospel and healing everywhere" (Luke 9:6).

"But," we may think to ourselves, "after all, they were the Twelve; perhaps this ministry of power is part of the apostolic call — certainly it is not for us." Jesus, however, delegated this same ministry to the Seventy, saying to them, "Heal the sick . . . and say to them, 'The kingdom of God has come near to you'" (Luke 10:9). And the Seventy did exactly as they were told, and they return thrilled, saying "Lord, even the demons are subject to us in your name!" (Luke 10:17). These were ordinary people, yet they were entrusted with extraordinary power.

Finally, we are given those startling words of Jesus in the Upper Room; "Truly, truly, I say to you, he who believes in me will also do the works that I do; and greater works than these will he do, because I go to the Father" (John 14:12). There is no way to get around it: the ministry of power is the common property of the people of God.

"OFFICIAL-LESS" POWER

This is nowhere more evident than in the book of Acts. How little the disciples really understood the matter of power, even after the resurrection, is seen in their initial question to Jesus, "Lord, will you at this time restore the kingdom to Israel?" (Acts 1:6). They wanted a kingdom so they could exercise a little power. "Is this the time when we can have the kingdom, the authority, the position, so we can really show those Romans what power looks like?" But Jesus made it quite clear to them that the matter of the kingdom was none of their business; he would give them power, spiritual power: "But you shall receive power when the Holy Spirit has come upon you; and you shall be my witnesses in Jerusalem and in all Judea and Samaria and to the end of the earth" (Acts 1:8). He gave them power without a kingdom, power without a position.

We are so often just like the disciples. We think the position guarantees the power. Give someone a Ph.D., a professorship, and then he or she will be able to teach! But we all know people with Ph.D.'s and professorships who cannot teach worth a lick. The position does not guarantee that the power is there. The world is full of people who will do anything to get the position so they can have power over others. That is the kind of power that belongs to this world system. It is dependent upon human authorization, and its power is the power to dominate others.

But to the eye of faith positions in the human order themselves are really powerless, ignorant of the way of God and the life of spiritual power. Throughout the book of Acts, we see repeatedly the clash between powerless officials and official-less power.

The authority of Peter, John, and the others was shocking to everyone because they had no human credentials of authority. They had no degrees, no titles of distinction, no human authorization. Since their ability (power) came from God, human authorization was irrelevant. Hence their authority flew in the face of the vested interests of those in power. Since the disciples had no need to be authorized, they could not be controlled.

Here we see uneducated common people standing before the "powerful" declaring, "Whether it is right in the sight of God to listen to you rather than to God, you must judge; for we cannot but speak of what we have seen and heard" (Acts 4:19–20). Here we see "officialdom" powerless to stop the healing of the sick and the preaching of the good news. Repeatedly, the official-less power of the disciples confronted the powerless officials of the religious and civil establishment, and repeatedly they won. They won because they operated out of a power that came from above.

One of the most humorous contrasts between human systems of power and spiritual power occurred in the ministry of Paul. He had been casting out many demons and in general exercising a ministry of power. Some professional Jewish exorcists saw Paul's work and decided to use his "technique," so at the next opportunity they tried to exorcise a demon, saying, "I adjure you by the Jesus whom Paul preaches" (Acts 19:13). But instead of obeying, the evil spirit answered, "Jesus I know, and Paul I know; but who are you?" And according to the Scripture, the man with the evil spirit "leaped on them, mastered all of them, and overpowered them, so that they fled out of that house naked and wounded" (Acts 19:15-16). What a contrast between official-less power and powerless officials!

HIDDEN PREPARATION

If we expect to engage in the ministry of power, we must understand the hidden preparation through which God puts his ministers. Moses thought he would set the world's wrongs right by the use of human power when he killed an Egyptian. What he thought would be creative power was in the end destructive power. There was a hidden preparation that was essential before Moses was ready for the ministry of power. He had to go into the desert for forty years to learn the difference between human manipulation and divine power. By the time Moses stood before God at the burning bush, he was a different man. Gone was the self-assured arrogance of one who could wield power with the wave of his hand. Now we find the meekest of human beings, who learned confidence by trusting in the power of God alone.

The apostle Paul also experienced a hidden preparation for his ministry. He was converted in dramatic fashion on the road to Damascus and later escaped his would-be assassins via a bucket dropped over the wall. He disappeared into the deserts of Arabia for three years, and after a brief visit to Jerusalem, fled to his old hometown of Tarsus for a number of years (Gal. 1:15-18; Acts 9:30; 11:25-26). It was nearly thirteen years from the time of Paul's conversion until he came to Antioch, where he began his missionary career. When we see in the book of Acts the great work of Paul, we must remember the hidden preparation that preceded it.

Today we have forgotten the importance of this hidden work of God. As a result, we immediately thrust people into notoriety, bestowing on them unbelievable power, and then we wonder why they are corrupted. Unless we are ready for it, power will destroy us. This is no small matter in the Church today. Because of our wholesale ignorance of the importance of hidden preparation, we have thrust untold numbers of workers into the limelight before they were ready.

All of us must experience this hidden preparation. Time spent being instructed by God is well spent and never wasted. In hiddenness we learn to see life spiritually—to see what is important and what is of little consequence. Often God completely reverses our priorities.

What we once saw as great and wonderful shrinks down to trivial and insignificant. Gaining recognition, success, wealth, and autonomy no longer attracts us. We learn to let go of all humanly initiated bids for power. Things we once considered unimportant and beneath us become matters of genuine consequence. We begin to value simple acts of kindness and neighborliness. Small ordinary tasks become genuinely significant to us.

THE MINISTRY OF SMALL THINGS

In experiences of hiddenness we learn that the ministry of small things is a necessary prerequisite to the ministry of power. Tabitha was a woman "full of good works and acts of charity" who gave her life to making "coats and garments" for the widows (Acts 9:36-42). She was exercising the ministry of small things. Barnabas shared his wealth with the struggling community, befriended Paul when others had given him the cold shoulder, and patiently nurtured John Mark when even Paul had decided he was unreliable (Acts 4:36-37; 9:27; 15:36-41). Barnabas too was exercising the ministry of small things.

When the people asked John the Baptist what they should do to exhibit true repentance, he counseled, "He who has two coats, let him share with him who has none; and he who has food, let him do likewise." To tax collectors he said, "Collect no more than is appointed you." To soldiers he counseled, "Rob no one by violence or by false accusation, and be content with your wages" (Luke 3:10-14). The point of his teaching is its triviality—small, simple ordinary things. John was calling people to the ministry of small things.

The ministry of small things is among the most important ministries we are given. In some ways it is more important than the ministry of power. The work of power occurs now and again, but the work of small things occurs repeatedly throughout the course of our days. Because our daily tasks afford us constant opportunity to engage in the ministry of small things, it is through this work that we become most intimately acquainted with God. No doubt this is one reason the prophet Zechariah counsels us not to despise the day of small things (Zech. 4:10).

Small things are the genuinely big things in the kingdom of God. It is here we truly face the issues of obedience and discipleship. It is not hard to be a model disciple amid camera lights and press releases. But in the small corners of life, in those areas of service that will never be newsworthy or gain us any recognition, we must hammer out the meaning of obedience. Amid the obscurity of family and friends, neighbors and work associates, we find God.

And it is this finding of God, this intimacy with God, that is essential to the exercise of power. The ministry of small things must be prior to and more valued than the ministry of power. Without this perspective we will view power as a "big deal." Make no mistake, the religion of the "big deal" stands in opposition to the way of Christ. It is this spirit that leads to the cruelest excesses. It is one of the greatest hindrances today to a free exercise of the ministry of power.

When power is seen as a "big deal," we want to draw attention to what we have done. We put up our signs and carry on our advertising campaigns in a frantic attempt to show that we are important. The one thing we cannot abide is for this great work of God (and ourselves) to go unnoticed.

The Bible tells us that after God used Peter to raise Tabitha from the dead Peter "stayed in Joppa for many days with one Simon, a tanner" (Acts 9:43). Now, what would we do if God had just used us to raise someone from the dead? I know what most of us would do: first we would go on a speaking tour, and then we would write a book about it! But Peter was content to do nothing, because he had no need to impress anyone. Power was no "big deal."

The ministry of small things can save us from the distortions of the "big deal." Under its authority power assumes its proper place as simply another normal aspect of the work we are given to perform. Power takes on a certain naturalness—the thing one would expect to see among the people of God—and it is experienced and reported in modesty and with humility. If small things become a glad and frequent ministry, we will discover that God is near us, and then the exercise of power will be a blessing and not a curse. Jean-Pierre de Caussade writes, "To discover God in the smallest and most ordinary things, as well as in the greatest, is to possess a rare and sublime faith."[1]

THE ALONENESS OF SPIRITUAL POWER

Those who exercise spiritual power must be prepared for aloneness. Please note that I did not say loneliness, for such persons will have many clamoring for their attention. Aloneness means having to decide and act alone, for no others can share the burden or even understand the issues involved. Wise counselors, friends, the community of faith—all are helpful, but only to a certain point. Most people have good intentions, but they simply do not understand spiritual power, and it is neither kind nor wise to ask them to help with decisions they can neither understand nor appreciate. We walk alone—well, not quite alone, for we have One who walks with us, but alone as far as human wisdom is concerned.

One of the most touching themes in the Gospels is Jesus' aloneness. The multitudes could not understand; even the disciples were thick of head and heart. Jesus tried to bring the Three—Peter, James, and John—along with him into the inner sanctuary of power, but they seldom could follow. They missed the whole point of the experience on the Mount of Transfiguration and could only think of how to set up an appropriate memorial. Most poignant of all is the scene in the garden of Gethsemane where Jesus singled out the Three to watch and pray with him. On that holy night they abandoned their Master for sleep, and Jesus was forced to wrestle with the powers alone.

We too must wrestle alone. We cannot even depend upon our husband or wife to understand what is occurring in the inner sanctuary of our soul. More than three hundred years ago James Nayler wrote of the aloneness of divine intimacy and power, "I found it alone, being forsaken. I have fellowship therein with them who live in dens and desolate places in the earth, who through death obtained this resurrection and eternal holy life."[2] Aloneness is the price of spiritual power.

THE PRACTICE OF POWER

It is one thing to applaud a true life-giving ministry of power and to see biblical models of power that take our breath away; it is quite another to experience spiritual power in our lives. The issue of real importance is how to bring the lofty talk into daily walk. What are some of the arenas in which the ministry of power needs to be exercised?

I want to be very straightforward with you in describing the first arena. We are to do battle with the Devil, Beelzebul, Apollyon, the Prince of the power of the air. Like Jesus, we go into the desert to meet the demons of the spirit, and if we do not go into a physical desert we do journey into the desert of the heart. We must not assume that we have fought this battle just because we have come into a living experience of faith in Jesus Christ, or just because we have been Christians for many years, or just because we have been active church leaders.

We need divine protection before daring to enter this dark night of faith. We ask for the strong light of Christ to surround us, the blood of Christ to cover us, and the cross of Christ to seal us. As we go into the desert of the heart, we enter with confidence, knowing that God is with us and will protect us.

But we go to the desert to meet, not God, but the Devil. In the desert we are stripped of all our support systems and distractions so that, naked and vulnerable, we face the demons without and within. There in the desert, alone, we look squarely into the face of the seductive powers of greed and prestige. Satan tempts us with wild fantasies of status and influence. We feel the inner pull of these fantasies because deep down we really do want to be the most important, the most respected, the most honored. We fancy ourselves before the cameras, in the judge's seat, at the top of the heap. "After all," we muse, "aren't these things nothing more than the desire for excellence?"

But in time we see through the deception. With a power given from above we shout, "No!" to him who promises the whole world if we will only worship him. We crucify the old mechanisms of power—push, drive, climb, grasp, trample. We turn instead to the new life of power—love, joy, peace, patience, and all the fruit of the Spirit.

Another arena in which the ministry of power needs to be exercised is the physical body. Many of us have so etherealized our spirituality that it is a genuine surprise to us to discover that the body plays an integral part in the life of faith. With the word of power we take authority over our bodies. We discipline the body so that it enters into a working harmony with the spirit. We bring the body into the God-given rhythms of life—eating, sleeping, working, playing.

Inordinate passions are like spoiled children and need to be disciplined, and not indulged. Sexual yearnings that transgress God's revealed will are controlled by the power of the Spirit. Slothful tendencies are restrained, tenderly but firmly. The same is true for a superheated zeal for work. Through prayer and faith we make food our servant and not our master. In the power of God we stoutly refuse to delay sleep at night in the pretense that our bodies are invincible. We exercise for health and spiritual alertness.

The healing ministry is part of the authority we are to exercise over our bodies. Jesus healed, and he commissioned us to heal (Mark 16:15-18).* Healing is listed among the spiritual gifts, and there is every indication that it is a valid ministry for today (1 Cor. 12:28). In our day, however, this good ministry has been abused terribly.

Some, for example, posit an absolute dichotomy between healing through medicine and healing through prayer. This is unfortunate and unnecessary! God uses his friends the doctors, who utilize their God-given knowledge and talents to bring health and wholeness. God also uses his friends who know how to pray to bring his life-giving power into hurting humanity. When doctors and nurses and other healing professionals learn to combine prayer with their medical skills, great good can be accomplished.

Another tragic abuse in the healing ministry is the tendency to assign blame if healing does not occur. We blame God, we blame ourselves, we blame the person who is sick. Often, for example, people will tell the per-

* I am aware that the authenticity of this passage is disputed, but it is quite consistent with Jesus' other statements and the experience of the church as recorded in Acts.

son who is ill that healing has not occurred because there is sin in his or her life. This is the worst possible counsel and is deeply destructive to the sick person, who wants nothing more than to get well. When the disciples tried to play this guilt game on the man blind from birth, Jesus quickly put a stop to it (John 9:1-3). For the most part, the issue of who sinned is simply beside the point; loving concern for the person is the point. May God raise up many who will bring to the healing ministry a compassionate heart and a good dose of common sense!

At this juncture I want to speak directly to those who have bodies that are frail or in other ways incapacitated. Be tender with yourself—slow to condemn, quick to encourage. Remember that spiritual power is as often gentle as it is dramatic. Give thanks for whatever physical abilities your body may have and concentrate on strengthening those rather than deploring your body's disabilities.

Pray for wholeness and well-being, and rejoice in whatever good comes from that process. If you have asked for healing and it has not come, do not fall into self-pity or self-condemnation. Keep praying, if you can, and remember that healing comes in many ways. Do your best to treat your body as a friend, not an enemy, and certainly in the resurrection, if not before, you finally will have a body that truly is a friend.

A third arena in which we need the exercise of spiritual power is the Church. In recent decades true power has been stifled by entrenched bureaucracies and a system of pastoral training that produces scribes rather than prophets. In order to have more freedom, many para-church organizations have sprung up, but these seldom have any mechanisms for accountability and usually end up being dominated by a single individual. As a result, we have, in the main, timidity in the churches and egotism in the para-church movements.

What is needed is a new renaissance of leadership

within the Church. We need churches who will call out their most capable men and women for ministry. We need seminaries who will train pastors to walk with God. We need pastors who will hunger for God and who will seek the power of God more than they seek position.

We desperately need pastoral leaders who know God. Their leadership should be both compassionate and strong. They must lead us through a strong pulpit ministry; they also must lead us through compassionate spiritual direction. When their leadership is infused with the joyful power of the Holy Spirit, it is a blessing indeed.

There are many other arenas in which the ministry of power is urgently needed, but I shall confine my discussion to only one more. The state, the arena of politics, needs the life-giving ministry of spiritual power. All believers, but particularly those in democracies, are to call the state to its God-given function of justice for all people alike. We are to commend the state whenever it fulfills its calling and confront it when it fails.

When I speak of the state I am not just referring to national governments, though I certainly mean to include them. By the state I mean all those systems of human organization whereby we empower people to represent and serve the whole. School boards, regulatory agencies, state legislatures, public health organizations, city councils, courts, and many others are all part of the state.

We discern the "angel" of the state through meditative prayer. Contemplation and interior prayer are closely linked with any genuine awakening of a social conscience. Upon receiving insight we "speak truth to power," as the old Quakers used to say.

Where the state genuinely and indiscriminately provides justice for all, we gladly commend it and give it our support. But if the state fails in this, we are to confront it vigorously with every means consistent with the weapons of Ephesians 6. Prayer and fasting, mourning and lamentation are weapons in our struggle for truth, the truth of justice. Vigorous protest, nonviolent confrontation, and civil disobedience are also weapons at our disposal. We serve the state when we refuse to give in to its demonic perversions. The underground railroad was civil disobedience in the nineteenth century; the sanctuary movement is civil disobedience in the twentieth century. In both cases believers declare with Peter and John, "We must obey God rather than men" (Acts 5:29).

Civil disobedience must, however, be done within the confines of spiritual power. There can be no coercion and no retaliation, because it grows out of love, not hate. It eschews the human weapons of violence but instead resorts to the "violence of love"—a firm intransigence to oppression and injustice.[3] The object is to make the evil visible and to prick the social conscience of people.

I have not forgotten that one means of waging the fight of faith is by being a public servant for the state and exerting a Christian influence from within. It is an honorable path, and many have chosen it. May their number increase.

The path of the public servant, however, is fraught with dangers, and not just the ordinary dangers of moral compromise via financial or sexual temptation. The state by definition has been invested with coercive power (that is, it can *demand* obedience), and coercive power is fundamentally at cross purposes with spiritual power. This does not mean that a believer cannot serve in the state; but it does mean that there are likely to be times when the state will make demands of its public servants that violate the Christian witness to love, and at that point the believer will have to decide whether allegiance belongs to Caesar or to God.

BE VALIANT FOR THE TRUTH

Of all people, spiritual people know the dangers of power. The temptations to abuse are everywhere. Yet we must not back away. Christ calls us to the ministry of power. He will give us the compassion and humility to fulfill our ministry. George Fox wrote, "Let all nations hear the word by sound or writing. Spare no place, spare not tongue nor pen; but be obedient to the Lord God and go through the work and be valiant for the Truth upon earth."[4] It is Christ who calls us; he will also empower us.

13. The Vow of Service

A Christian is a perfectly free lord of all, subject to none. A Christian is a perfectly dutiful servant of all, subject to all.

—MARTIN LUTHER

Power is a genuine paradox to believers. We love it and we hate it. We despise its evil and appreciate its good. We would like to do without it, but we know it is part and parcel of human life.

Our ambivalence about power is resolved in the vow of service. Jesus picked up a basin and a towel and, in doing so, redefined the meaning and function of power. "If I then, your Lord and Teacher, have washed your feet, you also ought to wash one another's feet. For I have given you an example, that you also should do as I have done to you" (John 13:14–15). In the everlasting kingdom of Christ, low is high, down is up, weak is strong, service is power. Do you sincerely want to engage in the ministry of power? Do you want to be a leader who is a blessing to people? Do you honestly want to be used of God to heal human hurts? Then learn to become a servant to all. "If any one would be first, he must be last of all and servant of all" (Mark 9:35). The ministry of power functions through the ministry of the towel.

Service means saying no to the power games of modern society. We refute the voices that say, "It's O.K. to be greedy. . . . It's O.K. to look out for Number One. . . . It's O.K. to be Machiavellian. . . . And it's *always* O.K. to be rich."[1] We reject the use of power to dominate and manipulate. We discard the symbols of power and prestige that are used to intimidate others.

Service means saying yes to true power harnessed for the good of all. We affirm power that frees and liberates. We rejoice when power is used in the service of truth. Power made obedient to the purposes and ways of Christ is our delight.

Service means discerning the powers, engaging the powers, and defeating the powers. We serve people when we disarm evil and set the captives free. Through prayers and tears, fasting and lamentation, we wage the peaceable war of the Lamb of God against all that is contrary to God and his way.

Service means obedience. By obedience to the ways of God we come to know the heart of God. By entering the heart of God we are enabled to be of help to people. Wholeness reigns in us, which means effective service for others.

Service means compassion. Compassion puts us in touch with all people. "Compassion requires us to be weak with the weak, vulnerable with the vulnerable, and powerless with the powerless."[2] Compassion gives us the heart to serve others.

Service means "servant leadership."[3] Our management style focuses as much on meeting the needs of people as it does on getting the job done. We are able to bring out the best in others because we value them as individuals. Our leadership flows out of servanthood; our first and primary drive is to serve, and our desire to serve motivates us to lead.

THE VOW OF SERVICE WITHIN THE INDIVIDUAL

The vow of service within the individual begins and ends with obedience to the ways of God. Until the matter of our obedience is settled, we cannot be useful to others, for we will constantly be bringing to that relationship our own agenda, our own opinion, our own human, manipulative ways. A life of obedience ensures that service flows out of divine promptings rather than human ingenuity. "Obedience gives servanthood its deepest dimension."[4]

The words of Samuel to Saul speak to us with prophetic force, "Behold, to obey is better than sacrifice" (1 Sam. 15:22). The greatest of God's demands is not for us to do heroic deeds or to make great sacrifices, but to obey.

Gethsemane gives us the most intimate and anguished model of obedience that we have in the entire Bible. Great drops of sweat like blood fell from Jesus' brow as he uttered the deepest prayer of obedience known to human beings, "Father if thou art willing, remove this cup from me; nevertheless not my will, but thine, be done" (Luke 22:42). Jesus was not trying to get out of drinking the cup—his crucifixion—he was trying to be certain that the cup was God's will. The will of God, not the cup, was the absolute thing. If the cup had not been in the plan of God, to drink it would have been disobedience. This is why when Jesus was finally clear that the cup was the path of obedience he said, "Rise, let us be going" (Matt. 26:46). At every point and in every way, Jesus was the obedient servant who did absolutely nothing except in response to the divine prompting.

I hope you understand that Jesus' obedience flowed out of his intimacy with the Father. Often the idea of obedience conjures up in our minds a hierarchical world of impersonal superiors issuing inane orders that we must obey even if we find no rhyme or reason for them. But Jesus' obedience, and consequently ours, is of a different quality altogether. It is an obedience that flows out of the intimacy that cries, "*Abba*! Father!" There is an inner knowing that God's ways are not only right but good. Knowing by experience the goodness of rightness, we concur with the will of God. It is no order to obey but a divine yes to follow.

The word *obedience* comes from a Latin root that means

"to listen." The good news is that we can live in such intimacy with the infinite Creator of the universe that we can hear his voice and obey his word. And it is our intimacy with the true Shepherd that makes our hearing and obeying possible.

What does this have to do with the vow of service? Service severed from obedience degenerates into spiritual stardom. Service devoid of obedience says, "Look at how wonderful I am, doing all these kind and self-sacrificing things! Look at how much good I am accomplishing." Indeed, the spirit of martyrdom that pervades service that is not in obedience to God often becomes a subtle tool of manipulation. We begin to control others through our service. When this happens, service is transformed into a demonic power and is, in fact, an act of disobedience.

But service that flows out of obedience is of a different quality altogether. When "we discover that our obedient listening leads us to our suffering neighbors, we can go to them in the joyful knowledge that love brings us there."[5] Vainglory, manipulation, coercion are all gone. We can disregard our obsession about the results of our service, since the divine nod of approval is completely sufficient. We can be fully present to people because we know we are living in obedience.

THE VOW OF SERVICE IN THE FAMILY

If the vow of service is to function anywhere, it must function in the family. Within the family unit, the ministry of the towel must be mutual and reciprocal. Respect and compassion should permeate all acts of authority and submission in the Christian home.

How do we as parents serve our children? We serve them by providing purposeful leadership. Children need wise counsel and concrete guidelines. They need loving correction. To lead is to serve.

How do we as parents serve our children? We serve them through compassionate discipline. Children are rendered a serious disservice when we fail to establish reasonable but clear boundaries for acceptable behavior. An early bedtime is important because sleep is important. Good nutrition is important because our bodies are important. Household duties are important because self-worth and a sense of contributing to the welfare of the family are important. Discipline is no small task, but it is one way we serve our children.

How do we as parents serve our children? We serve them by giving them a growing self-government.[6] We need to train our children for increased independence. We do not serve them by placing them under rigid rules until they reach the age of eighteen and then shoving them out the door. Early on, we teach children how to disciminate good from bad. We walk with them through life's decisions, gradually giving them opportunities to learn from their own mistakes. At some point in their growing self-government—certainly by age twenty-one—we relinquish all parental authority. We are available for advice and counsel, but only if they ask for it. Providing the atmosphere for a growing independence is serving children.

How do we as parents serve our children? We serve them by being available and vulnerable. The cliché that it is not the quantity of time but the quality that counts is simply false. Quality in large measure depends upon quantity. We need to give time to our children, and when we are with them we need to be transparent. To go to a child and say, "I was wrong, I'm sorry," is not a sign of weakness but of strength.

How do we as parents serve our children? We serve them by respecting them. Observe any large gathering of people, and see how children are systematically ignored. Their opinion is neither sought nor appreciated. Indeed, afterward, most adults would not be able to name any of

THE VOW OF SERVICE / 233

the children in the room. We, however, make a point of getting to know children. We listen to what they say and value their contribution. We do not make light of their concerns. The loss of a puppy for a child, or the breakup of a romance for a teenager, is a matter of genuine consequence and should be treated as such.

How do we as parents serve our children? We serve them by introducing them to the spiritual life. If we can be vulnerable enough to share our own pilgrimage of faith, it will go a long way toward making the spiritual life real to our children. And it is our job to instruct them in biblical faith; it is a vital service we owe our children. We must not depend upon the church to do the job of teaching for us.

The obligations of service are reciprocal. How do our children serve us? They serve us by being obedient. They obey not just because the Bible says to obey but because it is good to do so. Children cannot always understand the reasons for what we ask of them, but they can always be assured that their best interest stands behind all we ask. They obey even when it hurts to obey, though, as we shall see presently, obedience cannot be given when it is clearly destructive to do so.

How do our children serve us? They serve us through respect. Respect is due the office of parent even though sometimes the person fulfilling that role is a great disappointment. Parents whose lives show that they are not deserving of respect place a terrible burden upon children, and it is often a cause for their stumbling (Matt. 18:6).

How do our children serve us? They serve us by meekly refusing to do what is clearly destructive. We parents need all the help we can get, and we can learn from our own children, if we are teachable. Children run a terrible risk when they engage in this ministry of service. They risk our anger, and, more importantly, they risk losing our love and support. We must always assure them by word and deed that our love for them is stronger and deeper than any temporary disagreement. It is an unconditional love that is not dependent upon what they do or do not do. The one thing that is more important than their obedience to us is their obedience to the Voice from above.

How do our children serve us? They serve us by caring for our needs when the dependency roles are reversed. For everyone, the time comes when Mom and Dad need help. Aging parents may need their children's financial help, and they need their emotional help. It is not wrong for children to place parents in a nursing home, but their responsibilites do not end there. They also need to give their time, their presence, their attention, and, most of all, their love. Children have an obligation to serve parents in this way. In Jesus' day people tried to get out of this service to parents with religious excuses (Mark 7:9-13). It did not work then, and it does not work now.

All that I have said about the vow of service between parent and child also applies to the relationship of spouse to spouse and child to child. We serve each other in the Christian family because we follow Him who took on the form of a servant (Phil. 2:7). In modern society, one place where a Christian witness to the grace of God is desperately needed is in the home. The vow of service can help realize this witness.

THE VOW OF SERVICE IN THE CHURCH

In the Christian fellowship some serve by leading, others serve by following, and all serve by compassionate caring. Authoritative leadership is essential in the community of faith. It is easy to forget this when we see leadership abused. When we witness people jockeying for position and clamoring for status and using their power to put others into bondage, we are tempted to throw up our hands and try to do away with leadership altogether. But an infantile anarchy in church life is no better than an oppressive dictatorship.

Jesus recognized the need for leadership, but he also gave it an unusual twist. "Jesus called them to him and said, 'You know that the rulers of the Gentiles lord it over them, and their great men exercise authority over them. It shall not be so among you; but whoever would be great among you must be your servant, and whoever would be first among you must be your slave; even as the Son of man came not to be served but to serve, and to give his life as a ransom for many'" (Matt. 20:25-28).

Leadership therefore is an office of servanthood. Those who take up the mantle of leadership do so for the sake of others, not for their own sake. Their concern is to meet the needs of people, not to advance their own reputations. Bernard of Clairvaux wrote, "Learn the lesson that, if you are to do the work of a prophet, what you need is not a scepter but a hoe."[7]

We need leaders with servant hearts. We earnestly petition the Bestower of spiritual gifts to raise up humble men and women to be apostles, prophets, evangelists, pastors, and teachers (Eph. 4:11). We need them, each one. Their authority comes from God, and it is recognized and affirmed by the community of faith. They are our spiritual directors, and we honor them as servants of Christ.

How do spiritual leaders serve their people? They serve them by learning the ways of prayer. People desperately need the ministry of prayer. Marriages are being shattered. Children are being destroyed. People are living in dark depression and misery. And we can make a difference if we will learn to pray. If we genuinely love people, we will desire for them far more than it is within our power to give them, and that will lead us to prayer.

Let me briefly speak directly to pastors and others in positions of spiritual leadership. Your people expect you to bring the ministry of healing prayer. When you go into a home and see people bowed low with the sorrows of life, it is the most natural thing in the world to lay your hands upon them in the sacramental way and pray for their wholeness. Do it with all the confidence and humility, with all the tenderness and boldness, at your disposal. If you will do this day in and day out with a deep dependence upon the Holy Spirit, you will be amazed at the results. Many times there will be substantial improvement, and sometimes the impact will be so dramatic that it feels like a resurrection—and in a way it is. We do not need to be frightened of the few times when no improvement is noticeable, for there are many other times when much good has been done.*

One caution: we must pray for people in the utmost simplicity and joy. We do not try to psychoanalyze them or to figure everything out. We do not even try to correct their theology. We simply invite the Lord to enter the mind and the heart and to heal them both and to restore the God-intended personality.

There have been many who have prayed for me over the years. I remember one individual especially. As a result of three days of fasting and prayer, I felt led to ask this man to come and pray for me. He came, but instead of praying he began sharing his own shortcomings and confessing his sins. I thought to myself, "What is he doing? I am the one in need; he is the spiritual giant," but I said nothing. When he had finished, he looked up at me

---

* As a rough estimate, I find that about 20 percent of those I pray with seem to experience no improvement in their emotional or physical health; another 20 percent experience a little improvement; about 50 percent experience significant improvement; and about 10 percent experience dramatic improvement or total healing.

and asked, "Now, do you still want me to pray for you?" He had seen into my heart. He knew that I had turned him into a spiritual guru. When he finally placed his hands on my head and prayed for me, it was one of the most profound experiences of my life! There was a deep settledness and centeredness, a firmness of life orientation, that entered me at that time, and it has never left. I remember that, without knowing anything of my secret hopes and dreams, he had prayed for "the hands of a writer." Spiritual leaders serve people when they pray for them.

How do spiritual leaders serve their people? They serve them by blazing the trail of inwardness.[8] People today are profoundly interested in the inward nature of the spiritual life. They are also hopelessly confused about what it all means and how it relates to biblical faith. Henri Nouwen says that today's spiritual leader needs to be "the articulator of inner events."[9]

Spiritual leaders must discern the spirits for people. "Test the spirits to see whether they are of God," counsels John (1 John 4:1). Not every supernatural experience is an encounter with the God of Abraham, Isaac, and Jacob, and we had better learn the difference. There is so much foolishness today, so much holy baloney. Spiritual leaders need to help their people distinguish the voice of the true Shepherd from the voice of the evil one.

But even more, leaders serve by plunging into the spiritual depths ahead of their people and interpreting those experiences to them. If by their vulnerability they help us understand some of the dangers and rewards in this interior life hid with God in Christ, then we who are more timid will be able to step out with confidence.

One older woman did this for me. She was the head of the nursery of a large hospital and also the chairperson of the elders in the little church where I pastored. She worked the night shift and would often stop by the church in the morning after work. She read voluminously and would pepper me with questions about the spiritual life, many of which I could not answer. Oh, I could give a textbook answer, but I had no answer from life. More importantly, she would try many adventures in prayer at the hospital and in the congregation, and we would discuss at length what it all meant. What does it really mean to be "in Christ"? How does prayer work? What is the prayer of quiet? The prayer of faith? The prayer of command? How does prayer change others? How does prayer change us? These and many other questions challenged our faith.

She would pray for the babies in the hospital that were in critical condition. She put her hands in the gloves in the incubator and would hold a child, praying, sometimes for an hour or more, and almost always the baby would live.

What was she doing? She was blazing the trail ahead of me and encouraging me to step out into the spiritual life. And so I did. I made many mistakes. Sometimes I would be too bold and run ahead of my leading. More often, I would be too timid and need to be encouraged to step out. At every point, mutual clarification of what was happening enabled us to distinguish between creative and destructive power. She had served me by blazing the trail of inwardness.

How do spiritual leaders serve their people? They serve them by compassionate leadership. People do not need someone who will stand over them and pontificate in authoritative tones about the meaning of life. They need someone who will stand with them and share their excitement, their confusion, their hurt. People need leaders who love them.

I once worked for a psychologist who embodied the meaning of compassionate leadership for me. He was a leader, no doubt about that. He could be very forceful when the occasion demanded it. But his leading drew its strength from his compassion. All of us on the counseling team sensed his love. His clients also felt his kindness and caring. No distant pity for him, no narrow sympathy, but an all-inclusive compassion. In staff meetings he would sometimes read the love hymn of 1 Corinthians 13 and then stop and shake his head as if overwhelmed by the words. He loved to speak to us about love and "the psychic power of change through love," as he put it. All of us on the staff saw the power of that love. Following his leadership was not a burden, but a delight because we knew he loved us.

How do spiritual leaders serve their people? They serve them by being what Henri Nouwen calls "contemplative critics."[10] We live in a disruptive, disoriented time. From the bosom of the Church must emerge perceptive prophets who can help us understand the world. (And I do not mean those narrow-visioned "prophets" who wag their tongues at every news event, certain that it heralds the dawning of doom and the coming of Antichrist.)

Nouwen writes, "The contemplative critic takes away the illusory mask of the manipulative world and has the courage to show what the true situation is."[11] Such leaders are "contemplatives" because the inner silences are necessary to have perspective on this present evil age. Such leaders are "critics" because evil must be named and clearly distinguished from the good.

One contemplative critic I know is a very busy, very good teacher. It is not just the knowledge he displays, which is considerable; it is not even the wisdom and insight that permeate his teaching, though this is immensely helpful. It is the bringing together of all these things with compassion and humility. We would often sit in his study, with its book-lined walls and the grand piano off to one side and talk about the events in the world—not just the big events but also simple, everyday things.

Once, for example, I recall him asking me, "Have you ever noticed how we heat our homes?" He proceeded without expecting me to respond, "There used to be a day when we really did have central heat—the fireplace. Now people can be in the same house all evening and never see each other. Do you realize how much the way we heat our homes affects our family life!" Casual comments like these would often release a flood of ideas in my mind that could take years to process. Repeatedly he helped me see the world with new eyes—he was, and is, a contemplative critic.

How do spiritual leaders serve their people? They serve them by living under authority themselves. Nothing is more dangerous than leaders accountable to no one. We all need others who can laugh at our pomposity and prod us into new forms of obedience. Power is just too dangerous a thing for any of us to face alone. If we will look at the abuses of power in the Church today, very often we will see that behind them is someone who has decided that he or she has a direct pipeline to God and therefore does not need the counsel and correction of the community.

It was no accident that the monastic response to the issue of power was the vow of obedience. (There is even evidence that this was the first of the monastic vows.) Now, we may not feel comfortable with the monastic vow of obedience, but we do need to find ways to live under authority. Living under authority does not necessitate a superior-inferior relationship. Very often it can take the form of mutual accountability. Pastors can gather a small cadre of trusted peers who can share the spiritual journey with one another. The old Methodist class meeting was a way of providing mutual support and accountability, and it could be a helpful model for us today.

I have a pastor friend who helped me in more ways than I can tell. We began meeting when I asked him to

teach me to pray. We had wonderful times together—
talking, laughing, praying. It was a loving environment
in which we could follow the counsel of James to "confess
your sins to one another, and pray for one another, that
you may be healed" (James 5:16). In a way, we were spiritual directors for each other, though in those days I had
never heard of the term. We were living under authority.

In the church, as in the family, the obligations of service run both ways. How do we serve our spiritual leaders? We serve them through glad obedience. Pastors and
other leaders are shepherds of the flock; it is their responsibility to help us find the path of faithful living. Their
word of counsel or correction or guidance needs to be
taken with utmost seriousness. They can be wrong, for
they are fallible human beings just like us, but wise leaders are quick to listen and slow to speak, so when they do
speak we need to listen. We need to be under their authority.

How do we serve our spiritual leaders? We serve them
through constructive criticism. Glad obedience is not
blind obedience. There are times when spiritual leaders
need our thoughtful and loving correction. This is a service too.

In the past when I traveled and spoke I sometimes
took a friend with me to keep me honest. He knew me
well, and if my stories were becoming exaggerated, it was
his business to correct me. Jesus said that a prophet is
without honor in his own country, but sometimes when
we are in a far country we have too much honor. My
companion helped me keep my perspective under the
overzealous praise of well-meaning people.

Ordinary common sense should guide the service of
constructive criticism. It should be done in privacy and
with tact. It should be accompanied with loving support.
It should always aim to build up, and not to tear down.

How do we serve our spiritual leaders? We serve them

through the ministry of prayer. Loving, joyful prayer in behalf of our leaders can do much. When I was a pastor I would ask people to come by any time and give me a "booster shot" of prayer. Now that I teach at a university I encourage students in the same ministry. I don't want people to come to my office only when they are angry or burdened with some great need. I want them to come also when they are doing quite well and would like to minister life to me. It is a wonderful ministry that they perform. People just cannot feel isolated and alone when they are surrounded with that kind of loving support. These are only a few examples of the many ways there are to serve leaders through the ministry of prayer.

THE VOW OF SERVICE IN THE WORLD

It is all well and good to speak of service within the warm confines of the home or the believing fellowship, but what about the rough and tumble of the world of business and politics? To be a servant in a culture predicated upon competition may not be easy, but Jesus never suggested that discipleship would be effortless.

How do we serve others in the world? We serve them by valuing their opinion. We serve them by acts of common courtesy. We serve them by guarding their reputation. We serve them by simple acts of kindness. We serve them by integrity of life. We serve them by honesty, truthfulness, and dependability.

These sound so simple that we are tempted to think of them as unimportant. Simple they are, unimportant they are not. If we will just reflect on those few people who have had significant impact on our lives, we will often discover individuals who have performed simple acts of goodness in our behalf. The friend who takes the time to listen to us, the teacher who encourages us, the boss who recognizes our potential, the spouse who loves us, warts and all—these are those who serve.

How do we serve others in the world? We serve them by preparing ourselves to lead and by accepting the opportunity to lead when it is offered. Our world is hungry for compassionate, servant leaders. Talk about a mission field! Changes in the world will be initiated by those who are on the inside of the great institutions and who seek to lead them into better performance for the public good. For example, I may make some small contribution to the quality of life in this city by standing on the outside of the institutional structures and critiquing them and bringing pressure to bear where I can, but it is the mayor who is really going to have an impact on this city. Corporations, universities, and government posts desperately need skilled leaders who can give them the stamp of their personal values. Sears, Roebuck, the largest merchandising company in America, was significantly influenced by the leadership of Julius Rosenwald, who brought "unusual humanness and trust" to that great institution.[12] Thousands of other institutions need that same kind of leadership.

But the leadership must be *servant* leadership. Servant leaders are people who are servants before they are leaders and will be servants when the tenure of leadership is concluded. In *Celebration of Discipline* I discussed the character of that servanthood. Here I want to stress that this servanthood is the core of who we are as persons. The vow of service has become so much a part of our very nature that the easy thing is to serve, the hard thing would be to keep from serving. Every action arises out of that foundation, including the desire to lead itself.

How do we serve others in the world? We serve them by providing "meaningful work" for employees and performing "honest labor" for employers. Robert Greenleaf, author of *Servant Leadership*, who devoted all of his working years to management positions in AT&T, suggests that the time is right for the emergence of a new business ethic. He writes, "The new ethic, simply but quite completely stated, will be: *the work exists for the person as much as the person exists for the work.* Put another way, the business exists as much to provide meaningful work to the person as it exists to provide a product or service to the customer."[13] Meaningful work is work in which people feel a sense of accomplishment. It is also work in which people feel that they are making a genuine contribution to the good of society. Business managers and institutional trustees serve by helping facilitate this sense of meaningful work. Employees reciprocate by contributing honest work, work that is as good as possible, work that is as productive as possible.

How do we serve others in the world? We serve them by a firm refusal to allow them to misuse and abuse us. To allow people to walk over us as one would a doormat is not service, but subservience. It is not healthy for us or for others. Service must not be identified with a false modesty or a Caspar Milquetoast personality. On the contrary, service resonates well with forthrightness and courageous action.

Therefore, if others try to walk over us and take advantage of our serving spirit, we stand up to the abuse. Our concern is not to defend "our rights," for we have already given those to God. Firmly, we press others to respect all people—including us—as fully human. The issues can be many and varied—low salary, heavy workload, lack of advancement—the resolve is always the same: never to be "thingafied."

THAT SOLITARY INDIVIDUAL

We have come a long way on our journey into the nature of legitimate power and greatness. At times we have wondered if power is too great a danger, too fraught with corruption, to ever be brought into the service of

Christ. But in the end we have discovered that power harnessed to service can be an immeasurable good in human society.

And so we take the risk. We lead, we parent, we serve —always remembering that we do not serve some nameless, faceless humanity, but "that solitary individual."*

There is an old story† of a young fugitive who was taken in by the people of a small village and given a place to stay. Eventually, however, enemy soldiers came and demanded to be told where the young man was hiding. When the people hesitated to tell, the soldiers threatened to destroy the village and kill every man, woman, and child by dawn if the man they sought was not turned over to them. Frightened, the people turned to their beloved pastor for guidance.

Torn between deserting his people and betraying the young man, the pastor went to his room and began reading his Bible in hope of finding an answer before dawn. He read all night, and finally, just before sunrise, he came to the words, "It is better for one man to die for the people, than for the whole nation to be destroyed" (John 11:50, Jerusalem Bible).

Trembling, the pastor walked outside and told the soldiers where to find the youth. As they took the fugitive away to be executed, the people in the village began celebrating and feasting because their lives had been spared. The pastor, however, did not celebrate with them. Instead he went to his room smitten with a deep heaviness. In the evening an angel appeared to him and asked, "What have you done?" The pastor replied slowly, "I be-

* The phrase is Søren Kierkegaard's. It was to "that Solitary Individual" that Kierkegaard dedicated his book *Purity of Heart Is to Will One Thing*.

† There are numerous versions of the story, but this particular one is drawn from Henri Nouwen's *The Wounded Healer* (Garden City, NY: Image Books, 1979), p. 25.

trayed the fugitive." "But didn't you know," said the angel, "that the fugitive you betrayed is the Messiah?" "No! No! No!" groaned the pastor, "I didn't know, how could I have known?" The angel spoke: "If you had set down your Bible and gone to the fugitive and looked into his eyes you would have known!"

The vow of service is first and foremost a vow to look into the eyes of that solitary individual. And perhaps, just perhaps, that look will keep us from betraying the Lord of glory. You see, service is not really charts and programs and elaborate strategies to serve humanity. No, it is looking into the fugitive's eyes.

It is easy for us to see enemy soldiers all about us, and their power looks so overwhelming that it threatens everything we hold dear. We become so preoccupied with the enemy that we never see the frightened look in the eyes of this little child or the far-off look in the eyes of that old man. In fact, we do not see them at all—all we can see is the threat to our own security. What we miss is the gaze of Christ.

The vow of service means to see that solitary individual. This is the way of Christ. This is the path of obedience. And I have discovered that regardless of where this path leads us or whatever difficult decisions it thrusts upon us, it is the path of life.

Epilogue: Living The Vows

> You are a Christian only so long as you constantly pose critical questions to the society you live in . . . so long as you stay unsatisfied with the status quo and keep saying that a new world is yet to come.
>
> —HENRI NOUWEN

The vows of simplicity, fidelity, and service are for all Christians at all times. They are categorical imperatives for obedient followers of the obedient Christ. They are the beginning point from which we explore the depths of the spiritual life and discover our mission in the world.

The vows prod us into seeking a deeper spiritual life. We turn our backs on the superficiality of modern culture and plunge into the depths by making use of the classical disciplines of meditation, prayer, fasting, study, simplicity, solitude, submission, service, confession, worship, guidance, and celebration.[1] We help each other move forward in the spiritual life by encouraging those who advance and by comforting those who stumble.

The vows call us to a vigorous social witness. We stand in contradiction to the dominant culture, which has given its soul to the vows of greed, permissiveness, and selfishness. We critique the empty values of contemporary society, and call it to joyful discipleship to Christ.

The vows call us to evangelism and mission-mindedness. They are not ideals that we keep to ourselves and retreat into our cloistered homes to enjoy; they are to be freely shared with all who confess Christ as Lord and King. We have an obligation to win the nations and all peoples of the earth in anticipation of that day when "every knee should bow . . . and every tongue confess

that Jesus Christ is Lord, to the glory of God the Father"
(Phil. 2:10-11).

The time is now for a great new movement of the
Spirit of God. Such movements have emerged in the past.
Think of Abba Anthony and the desert fathers, Bernard
of Clairvaux and the Cistercians, Francis of Assisi and the
Friars Minor, Martin Luther and the Reformers, George
Fox and the early Quaker evangelists, and John Wesley
and the Methodist circuit riders.

It has happened before: it *can* happen again. Such a
movement must be disciplined, evangelistic, socially rele-
vant, and unapologetically Christian. It must take with
utter seriousness the need for spiritual power to sustain
the life of faith and overcome evil with good. It must
combine courageous action with suffering love.

Perhaps the vows of simplicity, fidelity, and service
could form the common commitment of such a movement. The Church could spearhead such an effort by including the vows as the minimum basis for membership.
And the churches, if they are willing, could provide a
context for the living out of the vows.

May a new wave of earnest prayer sweep the community of faith to petition God for the emergence of such a
movement of the Spirit. May powerful servant leaders of
the apostolic mold rise up to lead us into new avenues of
faithfulness. May we be willing to be in the vanguard of
such a new movement toward Christ in our day.

Notes

Chapter 1. Money, Sex and Power in Christian Perspective

1. James O'Reilly, *Lay and Religious States of Life: Their Distinction and Complementarity* (Chicago: Franciscan Herald Press, 1976), p. 22.
2. I want to express my debt to Jim Smith for encouraging me to look at *The Idiot* in light of my work on money, sex, and power.
3. Fyodor Dostoevsky, *The Idiot*, trans. Constance Garnett (London: Heinemann, 1913), p. 569.
4. Letter to Apollon Maikov, January 12, 1868, quoted in Konstantin Mochulsky, *Dostoevsky: His Life and Work*, trans. Michael A. Minihan (Princeton, N.J.: Princeton University Press, 1967), p. 344.
5. Brother Ugolino di Monte Santa Maria, *The Little Flowers of Saint Francis*, trans. Raphael Brown (London: Hodder and Stoughton, 1985).
6. Ibid.
7. Leland Ryken, "Puritan Work Ethic: The Dignity of Life's Labors," *Christianity Today*, 19 Oct. 1979, p. 15.
8. Ibid., p. 16.
9. Ibid., p. 18.
10. Henri J. M. Nouwen, *Clowning in Rome: Reflections on Solitude, Celibacy, Prayer, and Contemplation* (Garden City, N.Y.: Image Books, 1979), p. 45.
11. Brother Ugolino, *Little Flowers*, p. 274.
12. Massachusetts Historical Society *Proceedings*, vol. 21, p. 123, as quoted in Edmund S. Morgan, *The Puritan Family: Religion & Domestic Relations in Seventeenth-Century New England*, rev. ed. (New York: Harper & Row, 1966), p. 64.
13. Ibid., pp. 62–63.
14. Francis J. Bremer, *The Puritan Experiment* (New York: St. Martin's Press, 1976), pp. 177–78.
15. Ibid., p. 177.
16. Brother Ugolino, *Little Flowers*, p. 75.
17. Leonardo Boff, *God's Witnessses in the Heart of the World* (Chicago, Los Angeles, Manila: Claret Center for Researches in Spirituality, 1981) p. 149, as quoted in Francis J. Moloney, *A Life of Promise: Poverty, Chastity, Obedience* (Wilmington, Del.: Michael Glazier, Inc., 1984), p. 152.

18. Thomas Hooker, *The Cambridge Platform*, chap. 4, par. 3, as quoted in Herbert Wallace Schneider, *The Puritan Mind* (New York: Henry Holt, 1930), p. 19.
19. Dostoevsky, *The Idiot*, p. 156.

Chapter 2. The Dark Side of Money

1. Quoted in Edward W. Bauman, *Where Your Treasure Is* (Arlington, Va.: Bauman Bible Telecasts, 1980), p. 74.
2. Quoted in ibid., p. 84.
3. Quoted in Bernard Gavzer, "What People Earn," *Parade Magazine*, 10 June 1984, p. 4.
4. Jacques Ellul, *Money & Power* (Downers Grove, Ill.: Inter-Varsity Press, 1984), pp. 166–68.
5. Quoted in Elizabeth O'Connor, *Letters to Scattered Pilgrims* (San Francisco: Harper & Row, 1979), p. 8.

Chapter 3. The Light Side of Money

1. Quoted in Bauman, *Where Your Treasure Is*, p. 73.
2. Ibid., p. 113.
3. Ibid., pp. 89–90.
4. Quoted in Dallas Willard, "The Disciple's Solidarity with the Poor," 1984 (unpublished paper), p. 15.
5. I am indebted to Lynda Graybeal for this insight into the grace of giving.
6. I am indebted to Dallas Willard for insights into the control and use of money.

Chapter 4. Kingdom Use of Unrighteous Mammon

1. Ellul, *Money & Power*, p. 94.
2. Quoted in Don McClanen, *Ministry of Money Newsletter* (Germantown, Md.: Nov. 1983), p. 4.
3. John Woolman, *The Journal of John Woolman and a Plea for the Poor* (Secaucus, N.J.: The Citadel Press, 1972), p. 41.

Chapter 5. The Vow of Simplicity

1. John Calvin, *The Institutes of the Christian Religion, Book II*, trans. John Allen (Philadelphia: Presbyterian Board of Publication, 1813), chap. 8, sec. 45.

2. Ellul, *Money & Power*, pp. 110–11.
3. O'Connor, *Letters to Scattered Pilgrims*, p. 7.
4. Ron Sider, *Rich Christians in an Age of Hunger: A Biblical Study* (London: Hodder and Stoughton, 1978), pp. 175–78.
5. My thanks to Don McClanen for insight on this giving principle.
6. William Law, *A Serious Call to a Devout and Holy Life* (Oxford: Mowbray & Co. Ltd, 1981), p. 60.
7. Quoted in Malcolm MacGregor, *Training Your Children to Handle Money* (Minneapolis: Bethany Fellowship, 1980), p. 111.
8. These ideas grew out of a visit I had with Don McClanen, Director of Ministry of Money.
9. Quoted in Goldian VandenBroeck, ed., *Less Is More: The Art of Voluntary Poverty* (New York: Harper & Row, 1978), pp. 172 & 223.

Chapter 6. Sexuality and Spirituality

1. Lewis B. Smedes, *Sex For Christians* (Grand Rapids, Mich.: Eerdmans, 1976), p. 47.
2. David Allan Hubbard, "Love and Marriage," *The Covenant Companion*, 1 Jan. 1969, p. 2. I am indebted to Dr. Hubbard for his insights both here and later in my discussion of the Song of Solomon.
3. David Allan Hubbard, "Love and Marriage," *The Covenant Companion*, 15 Jan. 1969, p. 4.
4. Saint Augustine, *The City of God*, vol. II of *The Nicene and Post-Nicene Fathers*, 1st series (Buffalo: The Christian Literature, 1887), bk. 14, chap. 18.
5. Derrick Bailey, *Sexual Relations in Christian Thought* (New York: Harper & Brothers, 1959), p. 59.
6. Quoted in Letha Dawson Scanzoni, *Sexuality* (Philadelphia: Westminster Press, 1984), p. 46.
7. Jeremy Taylor, *The Rule and Exercise of Holy Living and Dying*, rev. ed., vol. III of *The Whole Works of the Right Rev. Jeremy Taylor*, ed. Charles Page Eden (London: Longman, Green, Longman & Roberts, 1862), p. 63.
8. Edward S. Morgan, "The Puritans and Sex," *The New England Quarterly*, Dec. 1942, p. 607.
9. Smedes, *Sex for Christians*, p. 49.
10. C. S. Lewis, *Mere Christianity* (London: Fontana Books, 1970).
11. Frederick Buechner, *Godric* (London: Chatto and Windus Ltd, 1981), p. 153.
12. Smedes, *Sex for Christians*, p. 56.

13. E. Mansell Pattison and Myrna Loy Pattison, "'Ex-Gays': Religiously Mediated Change in Homosexuals," *American Journal of Psychiatry*, vol. 167, no. 12 (Dec. 1980), p. 1553.

Chapter 7. Sexuality and Singleness

1. Donald Goergen, *The Sexual Celibate* (London: S.P.C.K., 1976), p. 181.
2. Smedes, *Sex for Christians*, p. 128.
3. Derrick Sherwin Bailey, *The Mystery of Love & Marriage* (New York: Harper, 1952), p. 53.
4. Smedes, *Sex for Christians*, p. 130.
5. Bailey, *Mystery of Love & Marriage*, pp. 53–54.
6. Smedes, *Sex for Christians*, p. 210.
7. McCary, James, *Human Sexuality*, 3rd ed. (New York: D. Van Nostrand, 1978), p. 150.
8. "Autoeroticism," in *The Encyclopedia of Sexual Behavior*, ed. A. Ellis and Aborbanel, vol. I (New York: Hawthorne Books, 1961), p. 204.
9. Smedes, *Sex for Christians*, p. 246.
10. This diagram was first suggested to me by Walter Trobisch, though I have modified it somewhat. His discussion is found in *I Married You* (New York: Harper & Row, 1971), pp. 77–83.
11. Richard J. Foster, *Freedom of Simplicity* (London: Triangle, 1981), p. 137.
12. Heini Arnold, *In the Image of God: Marriage & Celibacy in Christian Life* (Rifton, N.Y.: Plough Publishing House, 1976), p. 161.

Chapter 8. Sexuality and Marriage

1. Arthur Cushman McGiffert, *Martin Luther: The Man and His Work* (New York: Century, 1910), p. 287.
2. See Helmut Thielicke, *The Ethics of Sex*, trans. John V. Doberstein (Cambridge: J. Clarke & Co., 1964), pp. 79–144.
3. I am indebted to Dallas Willard for the insights he has given me into the Christian basis for marriage, divorce, and remarriage.
4. Lewis, *Mere Christianity*.
5. Quoted in J. Allan Peterson, *The Myth of the Greener Grass* (Wheaton, Ill.: Tyndale House, 1983), p. 175.
6. I am indebted to C. S. Lewis for this analogy. See *Mere Christianity*.
7. Charles R. Swindoll, *Strike the Original Match: Rekindling & Preserving Your Marriage Fire* (Eastbourne: Kingsway Publications Ltd, 1983), p. 136.

Chapter 9. The Vow of Fidelity

1. Ashley Montagu, *Touching: The Human Significance of the Skin*, 2nd ed. (New York: Harper & Row, 1978), p. 166.
2. Scanzoni, *Sexuality*, pp. 60–62.
3. Thielicke, *The Ethics of Sex*, p. 90.
4. Charlie Shedd, *Letters to Karen* (New York: Avon Books, 1978), pp. 61–69.
5. Elizabeth Achtemeier, *The Committed Marriage* (Philadelphia: Westminster Press, 1976), p. 86.
6. Moloney, *A Life of Promise: Poverty, Chastity, Obedience*, p. 118.
7. C. S. Lewis, *The Four Loves* (London: Fontana Books, 1963), p. 140.
8. Smedes, *Sex for Christians*, p. 169.
9. Lewis, *Mere Christianity*, p. 102.
10. James B. Nelson, *Embodiment: An Approach to Sexuality and Christian Theology* (London: S.P.C.K., 1979), pp. 211–35. I am indebted to Dr. Nelson for the insights that follow.
11. Ibid., p. 213.
12. Ibid., p. 217.
13. Ibid., p. 219.
14. Ibid., pp. 220–21.
15. Ibid., p. 222.

Chapter 10. Destructive Power

1. The imagery that follows is adapted from a poem by Arthur Roberts entitled "The Age of Metal," in *Listen to the Lord* (Newberg, Ore.: Barclay Press, 1974), pp. 61–63.
2. Paul Tournier, *The Violence Within*, trans. Edwin Hudson (London: S.C.M. Press, 1978), p. 128.
3. J. R. R. Tolkien, *The Silmarillion* (London: Allen and Unwin, 1977), p. 8.
4. Cheryl Forbes, *The Religion of Power* (Grand Rapids, Mich.: Zondervan, 1983), p. 85.
5. Walter Wink, *Naming the Powers: The Language of Power in the New Testament*, vol. 1 (Philadelphia: Fortress Press, 1984), p. 5.
6. Roselle Chartock and Jack Spencer, eds., *The Holocaust Years: Society on Trial* (New York: Bantam Books, 1978), pp. 132–36.
7. Brother Ugolino, *The Little Flowers*, pp. 44–45.
8. John Woolman, *The Journal and Essays of John Woolman* (New York: Macmillan, 1922), p. 167.
9. Quoted in Thomas E. Drake, "Cadwalader Morgan—Antislavery

Quaker of the Welsh Tract," *Friends Intelligencer*, vol. 98, no. 36 (1941), p. 200.

10. Tournier, *Violence Within*, p. 119.
11. Quoted in Jacques Ellul, *The Technological Society* (New York: Alfred A. Knopf, 1970), p. xi.
12. Wink, *Naming the Powers*, p. 130.
13. Ibid., p. 86.
14. James Nayler, *The Lamb's War* (1658), in Hugh Barbour and Arthur Roberts, *Early Quaker Writings* (Grand Rapids, Mich.: Eerdmans, 1973), pp. 106–7.
15. C. S. Lewis, *The Screwtape Letters* (London: Fount Paperbacks, 1982), p. 17.
16. George Fox, *The Journal of George Fox*, rev. John L. Nickalls (Cambridge: Cambridge University Press, 1952), p. 19.

Chapter 11. Creative Power

Sherri McAdam, a former student of mine, wrote the sentence used as the epigraph on Chapter 11 on a final exam for the course "Pioneers in the Spiritual Life."

1. Dietrich Bonhoeffer, *The Cost of Discipleship*, trans. R. H. Fuller (London: S.C.M. Press, 1964), p. 7.
2. Quoted in ibid., p. 35.
3. M. Scott Peck, *The Road Less Traveled* (New York: Simon & Schuster, 1978), p. 286.
4. Moloney, *A Life of Promise: Poverty, Chastity, Obedience*, p. 128.
5. See Aleksander I. Solzhenitsyn, *The Gulag Archipelago*, trans. Thomas P. Whitney (New York: Harper & Row, 1973). See also Cheryl Forbes, *The Religion of Power*, p. 35.
6. See *The Power of the Powerless* by Jürgen Moltmann, trans. Margaret Kohl (San Francisco: Harper & Row, 1983).
7. Martin Hengel, *Christ and Power*, trans. Everett R. Kalin (Belfast: Christian Journals, 1977), p. 81.
8. Robert H. Schuller, *Self-Esteem: The New Reformation* (Waco, Tex.: Word Books, 1982), p. 15.
9. Jean-Pierre de Caussade, *The Sacrament of the Present Moment*, trans. Kitty Muggeridge (London: Fount Paperbacks, 1981), p. 22.
10. James Dobson, *The Strong-Willed Child* (Wheaton, Ill.: Tyndale House, 1978), p. 76.
11. Myron Rush, *Management: A Biblical Approach* (Wheaton, Ill.: Victor Books, 1983), p. 13.

Chapter 12. The Ministry of Power

1. Caussade, *Sacrament of the Present Moment*, p. 64.
2. *Christian Faith and Practice in the Experience of the Society of Friends*, London Yearly Meeting of the Religious Society of Friends, ed. (Richmond, Ind.: Friends United Press, 1973), No. 25.
3. Jacques Ellul, *Violence: Reflections from a Christian Perspective* (Oxford: Mowbray & Co. Ltd, 1978), p. 166.
4. Fox, *The Journal of George Fox*, p. 263.

Chapter 13. The Vow of Service

1. Michael Korda, *Success!* (New York: Random House, 1977), p. 4.
2. Donald P. McNeill, Douglas A. Morrison, and Henri J. M. Nouwen, *Compassion: A Reflection on the Christian Life* (Garden City, N.Y.: Image Books, 1982), p. 4.
3. See *Servant Leadership: A Journey into the Nature of Legitimate Power and Greatness* by Robert K. Greenleaf (New York: Paulist Press, 1977).
4. McNeill, Morrison, and Nouwen, *Compassion*, p. 35.
5. Ibid., p. 40.
6. Charlie Shedd, *Promises to Peter* (Waco, Tex.: Word Books, 1970), pp. 17–59.
7. Quoted in Richard J. Foster, *Celebration of Discipline* (London: Hodder and Stoughton, 1981), p. 110.
8. I am indebted to Henri Nouwen for the analysis that follows. See *The Wounded Healer* (Garden City, N.Y.: Image Books, 1979), pp. 25–47.
9. Ibid., p. 36.
10. Ibid., pp. 43–46.
11. Ibid., p. 45.
12. Greenleaf, *Servant Leadership*, p. 139.
13. Ibid., p. 142.

Epilogue

1. See Foster, *Celebration of Discipline*.

Scripture Index

Subject Index